THE DIGNITY

PROFIT

CREATING COMMUNITY THROUGH
ENTREPRENEURSHIP

NATHAN W. MCKIE, SR.

THE DIGNITY OF
PROFIT

Creating Community Through Entrepreneurship

NATHAN W. MCKIE, SR.

KS
Kravitz & Sons

Kravitz and Sons LLC
204 E Arlington Blvd. Suite B
Greenville, NC 27858

Published by Kravitz and Sons LLC.
ISBN: **979-8-89639-372-6** (sc)
ISBN: **979-8-89639-371-9** (e)

Library of Congress Control Number:

Contents

ACKNOWLEDGMENTS

I would especially like to acknowledge the members of a Christian study group that meets at Ridgecrest Baptist Church in St. Charles, Missouri, two times a month. Since 2002, I have been a part of this group that chooses to study a different book a couple of times each year. This group of men allowed me to use them as guinea pigs for the review of my manuscript. Most of them are not engaged in missions, so this was a real test to see if I could keep them interested for the approximately six months that it took to work through it. Not only did they do that, but they also made some great suggestions that materially changed my thinking about my approach.

Without them knowing it, there are several other groups or individuals who helped to shape my thinking about a new way to approach mission activity. First was Habitat for Humanity that offers homeowners a shared experience to help make their dreams come true. Second, Mountain T.O.P. in east Tennessee, a Christian organization, showed me that the Habitat format can be applied to a Christian mission trip experience. Third, Robert Lupton, whose works I have cited several times in the book, invested his life in revitalizing a blighted area of Atlanta and showed that involving entrepreneurs in the process is the only viable way to be successful.

None of what I have written would have the impact that I believe it will without the support of the Arcadia Valley Ministerial Alliance and the Iron County Economic Partnership in Iron County, Missouri. These folks have put their faith and trust in an innovative endeavor that can transform the way we deal with poverty and job and entrepreneurial training.

Virtually every citation used has helped to put me on the right path to hopefully solving some of the most endemic problems in rural America. It would be remiss of me to overlook the impact of each and every one of these sources.

Without a doubt, God has been involved in my work from the earliest stages. All my notions have clearly come from hints that the Holy Spirit dropped on me. Every time my encouragement seemed to wane, I felt the nudge through an idea that just fit the situation at the time. All the glory belongs to Him.

It seems to me that we are the product of all that we do, read, and observe. Taking what I have put forth and pursuing it further through the reading of some of these other sources will give you a perspective that will enable you to profit from doing the work of helping alleviate poverty.

DEDICATION

To the many "warriors" who trek to various locations around the globe to make the lives of people better, I dedicate this book. It has been a labor of love, and I did it because I am a strong advocate of the best utilization of resources in any endeavor I engage in.

The job these folks do is thankless in the sense of getting a direct reward for your efforts. The call of our God is full of rewards, just perhaps not in the worldly sense. The average person sees no reason for getting involved in such projects. My desire is to help interest many of the otherwise "uninterested parties" by showing them a different perspective and a different methodology.

In the end, we should be about doing good for others and helping others see the *profit* in doing so. That profit or benefit, if you will, should be the realization of the goal of helping people be able to do for themselves whenever possible. When we do that, we can achieve *the Dignity of Profit.*

Dignity (one of the gifts of business). The ability to create jobs that give people a sense of dignity and purpose, as well as a reason to get up in the morning, is one of the most important offerings of business.

Laurie Beth Jones

Jesus, Entrepreneur

PREFACE

Perhaps every Christian struggles with what it means to authentically live out the *Great Commission*. On the one hand, it seems that mission activity is external, either a special one-off experience "somewhere else" or a full-time job as a missionary. Integrating it into everyday lay life seems impossible.

It's not clear to me just when I began to feel that evangelical work made sense for me. When I got old enough to be on a church committee, I knew evangelism was not something that I wanted to do. My view of it was someone standing on a street corner wearing a sign that said something like: "Repent! The End is near!" I was incredulous as to why the people that I saw wearing those signs had that kind of knowledge. It just reeked of arrogance, and arrogance has never seemed like a good thing. It seemed like the Pharisees tried to get a corner on this kind of knowledge and make it hard for others to acquire it.

Since arrogance wasn't something that I wanted to be accused of, keeping any knowledge about the end times to myself didn't seem appropriate. Who wants to get into a religious argument unless you are trying to be Pharisaical? I certainly didn't. For me, that would be like taking a knife to a gunfight! In college, I was surprised when I actually had an answer that helped to bail out a young student who had gotten himself into a "discussion" with an agnostic. 1 Peter 3:15 tells us to be ready to give an answer, but that scares most of us.

Add to this background the opinion I had long held about *mission trips*. My kids went on them, and it seemed that they repaired houses for a while and then played. I didn't know much about the *Great Commission* in those days, so I just couldn't see the point. Mainly, it didn't appear that anyone was learning anything on these trips. Perhaps they were feeling good about the experience, but even adults who went mainly talked about everything except helping people find Jesus. My wife and I met while counselors at a church camp, but that's not the same. Admittedly, there are those young people who don't really care about what goes on at those camps if it doesn't involve entertainment. However, it is less threatening in that most of the kids don't know as much as the counselors do. What passes for evangelism mostly seems to be overshadowed by other activities.

There came a time (at least in the United Methodist Church) when *evangelism* became known as *outreach*. Shakespeare once said that "a rose by any other name smells as sweet." I guess the reverse can be true as well. We mostly hear people use the phrase: "it looks like a duck..." The bottom line is that most people still know what is going on and don't want to have any part in it. Churches now have staff that is known as being involved in *discipleship*. However, this is still not doing much to fulfill the *Great Commission*.

It would be misleading to leave you with the impression that any of this made any difference to me. It was my philosophy to just live my life as I believed Jesus wanted me to and let the chips fall where they may. As fate (or, more correctly, God) would have it, some events changed my attitude to the point where I was interested in making disciples. Well, at least I began to see my faith from a different set of eyes. What I found is God pursues us because he cares for us. He wants us to care for others, and the way we are to do that is to <u>show</u> them. After all, the saying is quite true that goes: "People don't care how much you know until they know how much you care."

When It All Began to Change

Like all change, it normally doesn't happen like a flash of lightning. I had avoided getting too deeply into my faith by saying that I didn't need a "Road to Damascus" experience. I was more correct than I thought at the time. Oh, there were events that started me down a different path, and those were the life-changers for me. I broke down and went to a Habitat for Humanity project. The first one was a stinker because there wasn't any meaningful work to do. We spent the day making name tags for the "Friends of Habitat" recognition banquet. Fortunately, that didn't put enough cold water on my attitude to keep me from trying again. The next experiences weren't much better until a group of churches went together to build a house. As I worked, I noticed that around us were houses built by a local bank and one by the St. Louis Cardinals baseball team. The owners didn't know the difference insofar as to why we were all there.

A youth leader at my home church took a group of youth to work at a project in Tennessee called Mountain T.O.P. (Tennessee Outreach Project). On the surface, this seemed like your "run of the mill" mission trip: rehabbing houses and having some fun while they were at it. When they came back and reported to the congregation about their experiences, I saw something that I hadn't seen before. I could see that their lives had been changed, but I also got a strong impression that the homeowners had their lives changed as well. I had to check it out for myself.

My first trip had me on a work team with the man who had founded the project 25 years prior. Once, when we were at our assigned house, I asked him what he thought made the difference in this project compared to others. He turned to the homeowner and said: "Miss Emma, tell Nathan what Mountain T.O.P. has meant to this area." Her response was: "Before this started, our county had the highest teen dropout rate and the highest teen suicide rate. What Mountain T.O.P. has done is to give us hope." I ended up going for four years straight – the last one by myself. Clearly, I had changed because of it. I now saw how these trips had done more than just make peoples' housing situations better; these people had their lives changed as well.

While studies offered at church and being involved with the Walk to Emmaus (see Chapter 1) had made certain changes in the direction my faith journey, I needed to have another nudge. While Mountain T.O.P. had given me a different view of mission trips involving house-building and repair, I was still not "all in" on the evangelism/outreach/discipleship things. What was missing was the connection between my Christian side and my work-life side. That change in direction came when I was selected to be the Missions Chairperson at a different church. I knew that they had been going on a trip each year, and this had been happening for 18 years! To further complicate matters, it was a far cry from what Mountain T.O.P. was about. I didn't really know about anything else, so I began to check out what else they were doing.

The rest of the story will come as I relate it during the telling of the message of this book. The tipping point actually came, though, when the Endowment Committee decided to make a major contribution to some local charities. The church, though lacking in other areas, was very generous with some charitable endeavors. The committee made their recommendations, but the church council decided to have the Missions committee decide on some alternatives and bring them back to the council. I did a lot of research, and this included learning about a small-business incubator run by a Catholic charity. It was a faith-based one, and it didn't compare with anything else I had witnessed. There had to be a connection to the mission of the ministry as a whole and showed how powerful an outcome-based approach could be. This became one of our beneficiaries, and it gave me the passion to do this type of project instead of housing projects.

The impact of these changes will be revealed throughout the rest of the book. It is my desire for you to see an exciting future where you can make a very important impact in other people's lives. This is some of the most important evangelism that you can do. It is directed at one of the significant needs in a person's life: having the *dignity* of being able to provide for themselves and their family.

This is why I chose the title, *The Dignity of Profit*. First, I want to help you prepare yourself to get engaged in making a difference in the way much of the charitable activity is conducted. As we begin to build on the idea of truly helping alleviate poverty, we can look at some ways this can actually be done using some unlikely missionaries – entrepreneurs.

INTRODUCTION

D r. Charles Stanley (Stanley 2008) has said that there are two types of people: those who are servants and those being served. Jesus even said that He came to serve (Matt. 20:28). Now, here is where the departure comes: even if we find ourselves on the right side (being a servant), there is a lot of debate about how we serve. It seems that we really differ on **why** we serve. So, if we take this into the context of *need-oriented evangelism* (Schwarz 2006, 36), we find a different motivation for our service.

Are you a servant? If so, who do you serve? OK, the easy answer is: "I serve the Lord Jesus Christ." Good, but that doesn't let you off the hook. In addition to the one cited above, He told his disciples that not giving water and food to the "least of these" was the same as not giving them to Him (Matt. 25:38-41). In the Parable of the Talents (Matt. 25:26), He referred to the servant who buried his one talent as "wicked and lazy." To me, this puts the matter in pretty clear perspective when he tells us how a servant should behave. Jesus modeled "right" behavior many, many times, and we should pay closer attention to that.

Why I Wrote This Book

1. I have been a member of thirteen churches and visited several others, and none of these were very concerned about the kingdom-related outcomes of their mission activities. One of them even has sent teams to the same area for over

1

CREATING COMMUNITY THROUGH ENTREPRENEURSHIP

THE DIGNITY OF PROFIT
CREATING COMMUNITY THROUGH ENTREPRENEURSHIP

25 years now. It has become a way to enjoy seeing and working with friends – not so much about the mission. I will have more to say about this later.

2. Business people do not feel welcome in certain denominations beyond showing up in worship services and making large contributions. Consequently, their contributions (financial and otherwise) are not as large as they could be. Most clergy (and some lay leaders) personify these feelings. In all of the churches I have been involved with, the membership of business people was much smaller than the rest of the other categories.

3. Some churches just aren't interested in *missions*. United Methodist churches are obliged to pay "apportionments" to their Conference organization, and that includes a portion for missions. When I was growing up, some churches would deduct amounts that were supposed to go to foreign missions from their payment to the Conference. Some members write on their offering checks that they don't want any of their "gifts" to go to missions. These aren't bad people; they just feel that the money goes to some people that they don't agree with.

4. Poverty robs people of their dignity. Giving someone something that they can and should acquire for themselves further reinforces that. When I have pointed this out to others, they don't seem to be aware of this. It should come as no surprise that much of what passes for charity is actually creating dependency.

5. The churches that are interested in doing something to address the needs of their members and others with regard to their economic situation aren't finding a plethora of opportunities to engage the ones that need help. This may, in large part, be due to the attractiveness of food pantries and the like. If they do find opportunities, they find it difficult to recruit volunteers to help.

6. Even those churches, benevolent organizations, and individuals who are interested in trying to "do the right

thing" are wasting billions of dollars by perpetuating dependency. Robert Lupton, in his first book *Toxic Charity* (Lupton 2011, 1-9, points out that the most common ways of trying to alleviate poverty are ineffective at best and downright harmful at their worst.

How we can change things

Nothing that has been around for as long as mission efforts have will be changed in a short period of time. David Smick, in *The Great Equalizer* (Smick 2017,193-195), suggests several ways that we can begin to undo some of the damage that has been done by those who refuse to realize that we are supposed to look out for someone besides ourselves. Smick and others have pointed out the problems we face as a country and around the world.

Now, I am not naïve enough to believe that anything that I do will make a big difference. A Chinese proverb says that a nation is secure when a man plants a tree that he won't sit under. This is a message about unselfishness and future-focused thinking and planning. In the end, it takes people who will "plant trees" to provide a payoff later.

Here's how I have laid it out in this book. It has a progressive pattern to it, one that provides a way for readers to prepare themselves by understanding the importance of the components:

1. A better understanding of the nature of mission service will include some of the prevailing opinions. This will also address the need to have businesspeople involved. This also means that we need to understand the balancing act we have to deal with in our lives. *Chapter 1*

2. Take a look at the importance of seeing *profit* as vital in having success in your endeavors. Jesus gave us the *Great Commission*, but he also gave us many lessons that give us a better understanding of being fruitful. *Chapter 2*

3. Attitudes are what drive our thinking and our acting. We consider how a better understanding of how focusing on them can enable us to do better planning in seeking to serve

others. *Chapters 3 and 4*

4. We will embark on a journey that has as its first stop a place called L.A.L.A. Land. This represents the main factors possibly causing a particular area to be facing stagnant or no growth. While there, we will consider some of the ways we can begin to deal with the problems created by this. *Chapter 5*

5. Our second stop is a place where we can better assess the impact of not being in *community* with our neighbors. My experience and research have led me to believe that progress is difficult, if not virtually impossible when people in a group situation do not have good relationships with one another. *Chapter 6*

6. At this stop we will also look at the importance of taking the proper steps to draw people together into the type of relationships that will work and can last. If we can't take the steps necessary to make this happen, we will be stuck here until we can find a way to make it happen or give up and go "home." It is here we will consider how to R.E.A.C.T. to find the way to the next stop. *Chapter 7.*

7. Hopefully, your next stop will be S.U.C.C.E.S.S. Valley. The results of your efforts will be revealed here (if you are successful) by the words making up this acronym. It is a model by which you can move forward on your current or future projects – if you can maintain the relationships that have developed. *Chapter 8.*

8. Having reached the previous stop, it is appropriate to look at some other ways to address some of the needs that arise. I recommend reading all the way through before you charge off in an attempt to solve your problem(s). It is easy to feel that you have found the answer you need when you have not been as correct in your assumptions as you need to be.

9. The final chapter, *Moving Forward*, will help you reflect on what has been presented in order to begin the planning phase. The Appendices provide an expansion of most of the main topics presented in the book. You are welcome to visit

any of them whenever you choose, but please refer to the ones you feel a bit inadequate to handle once you have read all the way through. *Chapter 9.*

10. There are many citations throughout the book. I didn't do this to be a name dropper; there have been a lot of authors that have helped shape my knowledge base about some of the principles I have shared. There are many Bible passages because this topic has been driven by the words of the Holy Scriptures. Everything important in life is addressed in them, although some discernment must be used to determine how to interpret them. The reason I have cited them is that I hope you will research them for yourself to expand your understanding of what they have presented.

11. Although the strength of my message comes from my experience and the depth of my passion for doing *missions* well, the stories and opinions have been kept to a minimum. This is an attempt to avoid any bias in the presentation. If you don't agree that I have succeeded in my attempt, I hope you will take them with a grain of salt and allow me to try to be convincing.

Each person approaches the challenges they face for different reasons and with different levels of aptitude. It is my desire for you to be encouraged to do what you can to help alleviate poverty by empowering people to "take the bull by the horns." All of this has to be at the direction and the guidance of the Holy Spirit. During your reading, continue to be in prayer and be open to what Jesus wants you to know as you embark on this important *mission.*

What Does It Mean to Restore Dignity?

Perhaps you don't think much about what it means to have *dignity*. We refer to situations as being dignified or not, and that has a lot to do with it. In reality, much of what we have that makes us dignified is outside our control. For instance, you may find yourself struggling to make ends meet (welcome to the world of reality). Maybe you have a debilitating disease that makes you unable to do things most *normal* humans can do with ease. These may be due to circumstances you had no part in.

Merriam-Webster defines *dignity* as the "quality or state of being worthy, honored, or esteemed." An extension of this includes "a sense of pride in oneself, self-respect." It always tends to make me feel uncomfortable when I am around people who don't care enough about how they are viewed by others to dress or act as if they do care.

It has been said that you can "get bitter or get better." It all has to do with *attitude*. We will deal with that extensively in Chapter 5. Attitude has a lot to do with how you view the world. That one is in Appendix G, but you don't have to be focused on your *worldview* to have an *attitude*. Once upon a time, it was common to say that a person had "copped an attitude" or to tell someone that they "shouldn't get an attitude." Guess what: we have an attitude whether we "get one" or not.

Back to *dignity* **– our** *attitude* **strongly affects how we view dignity.**

I personally have seen a lot of people who are in dire circumstances or have a very deformed body who have more dignity than a rich, privileged person of "high esteem."

You probably have to, if you think about it. My guess is they didn't think much about their *dignity* before they found themselves in that situation. How they feel about it now has everything to do with how they view the world.

You will find that the road to *indignity* has a fairly well-defined path. This is spelled out in Appendix E as we look at the risk involved in working with people whose dignity has been sucked out of them. To a great extent, people's attitude about what is happening to them is what leads them to lose their dignity – or maybe not.

THE DIGNITY OF PROFIT

Part I:

Why Should We Be Doing This?

CHAPTER 1

PREPARATION FOR THE JOURNEY

For forty years, I lived my life in complete ignorance of what God wanted me to do. My attitude about God was: He is in control of the universe (things like floods, tornados, etc.), and I would be in charge of me. That sounds arrogant, but I felt like it was presumptuous to expect that God wanted to have to tend to my issues.

It is important for each of us to understand how we think about God if we want to determine how best to serve Him. I suggest that you take a Spiritual gifts assessment. It was one of the most liberating events that I have ever encountered. I have done it several times, and each time gave me some different insights. Mainly, you can find out what you don't have to feel guilty about.

Having said all of that, I need to contradict myself somewhat. Christian Schwarz, creator of the Natural Church Development (Schwarz 2006, 36) program, points out that not everyone has the gift of evangelism. He goes on, however, to say that it doesn't mean we are not to be evangelistic, at least not in the way that we typically think. According to his analysis, we all are supposed to be reaching out to the unbeliever when we are presented with the opportunity. Earlier, I mentioned that 1 Peter 3:15 tells us we are always to be ready to give an answer for the hope within us.

If you have ever thought you would like to know what God's will is for you, you probably experienced some frustration in trying to find out. Dr. John MacArthur (MacArthur 1972) wrote a book that helped me a lot several years ago when I was struggling with it. The title of it was *Found: God's Will*, but I had to read it twice to get the point. What it boils down to is there are several things you can do to get yourself into a position to receive the message. None of these included sitting around waiting for God to speak to you out of Heaven or anything like that. Elijah found out how subtle God is when he hid in a cave (1 Kings 19:1-12). Elijah was hiding from Jezebel, and God came and asked him what he was doing. Now, God knew what Elijah was up to, but he wanted Elijah to experience how God speaks to us – the still, small voice. Elijah's heart had to be ready as ours does.

We Are Called

We all know what a *call* is in a general sense. Most of the calls we get are ones that we can take or leave. Certainly, a call from God should be taken seriously, but most of us don't really understand that it is. Those who God calls (saves), He commissions. This is most commonly stated in Jesus' words in Matthew 28:18-20: "…Go therefore and make disciples of all nations, baptizing them in the name of the Father, and the Son, and the Holy Spirit…"

There is what is known as a *general call*. This is a call to the gospel, as we see in Matthew 22 words, "Many are called, but few are chosen." The one that is more significant for us to consider is what is known as the *effectual* or *efficacious* call. This is to the church or assembly of those called, summoned as believers. I'd like to leave it at that before I get into trouble.

Getting back to *God's will*, it can be inferred that since it is not His will that any should *perish* (2 Peter 3:9), His will is for us to respond to His call. His will is to be done, and it will be done. Before I plunge into circular reasoning, let me say that God does have a plan. Who ultimately participates in it getting done depends on a lot of things. Suffice it to say paying attention to His call means that we love Him and want to be obedient. So, let's look at some of the components in His call.

We are Called to Accept Our Commission

The receipt of my *commission* as a Second Lieutenant of the U.S. Air Force was a very special time for me. Signed by the President of the United States, it was confirmation of my passing the requirements for the commission, and I was then ready to serve my country in that special way.

A call from God is our commission as Christians. As in the military, one must become equipped for the task.

I went into pilot training, which was my way of becoming equipped for the task ahead. When I was disqualified for physical reasons, I went to Supply Officer training so I could do that for the rest of my time on active duty.

You may have heard it said that "God doesn't call the equipped; he equips the called."

By accepting God's call, we become "commissioned" to serve Him, and by doing so, we will be equipped to do His will.

We Are Called to Be Faithful

You may have heard it said: God doesn't ask us to be successful; He calls us to be faithful. There is some truth to that, but it is a bit too easy to go charging off on some project that possibly shouldn't be done anyway. It just doesn't seem we are being faithful if we are ignoring or misinterpreting our "call." My maternal grandfather was a minister, and he used to say a lot of preachers must have heard something a bird chirped and thought was their *call.* I have run into a lot of folks that go on mission trips and get drawn in by people who are in a dependency mode. Later in this chapter, you will find an introduction to that point when I discuss *discernment.* The credibility that comes from being faithful and dependable is priceless. Jesus put it pretty simply when He said: "Let your 'yes' be 'yes' and your 'no' be 'no'" (Matt. 5:37). It is amazing how many people today find it difficult, if not impossible, to follow through on what they have agreed to do.

Faithfulness usually gets connected to our obligation to our

Christian beliefs or to some cause. The important point in this case is faithful people are usually dependable. After all, we aren't being faithful if we can't be depended on when it counts. Integrity means that there is "one way," and we are called to have it as Christians.

We Are Called to Be Obedient

One of my favorite hymns is: "Trust and Obey." Obedience is usually thought of as adherence to rules. People have referred to the Bible as a "book of rules." Actually, it is a book of truth. So, being obedient really means living in the truth of God's Word. As I alluded to in the previous section, being dependable means we are faithful. There may be a fine line between being dependable and being obedient, but the point is our obedience to Jesus' commandments means we are being faithful and dependable.

Jesus said if we love Him, we will do His commandments (John 14:15). That is one of those "simple, but not easy" statements. Some of us find it hard to be *obedient*. It may be that we are just hard-headed or stiff-necked, as it was referred to in Scripture. If you think about what happened to those folks the Bible talks about; you may find a crowd you don't want to be a part of. Discipline is a challenge to some, and that can be good sometimes. What matters is where your heart is. It has been said the longest journey is from the heart to the head (mind). The heart is what God wants, and that can help us to be obedient.

We Are Called to Be Disciples and to Make Disciples

As Jesus was making some of His last statements on earth, He included one of the most important ones: the Great Commission. The operative words are in Matthew 28:19, where he says to His disciples that they are to "…make *disciples* of all the nations…" He didn't say to make friends or to make church members. There's nothing wrong with that, except just being a friend or a fellow church member won't get the job done. After all, being a disciple means we "…should love one another." (John 13:35).

Dr. John MacArthur (MacArthur 1988) describes what this means as he describes divine love as being *sacrificial*. Here's what he has said about it: "It's the love of choice. And it's a love that is expressed in meeting a need, doing a deed of kindness, caring for someone in a practical way, and humbly serving others. That's the kind of love it is. It's not the love of a feeling; it's the love of action. It is not really an emotion, although emotion will come along."

So, why don't we do it more often if it is so easy? That's probably a complicated question in some ways, but it really is that simple to carry out. Married people have to understand how to be a servant to their spouse, or they will have lots of problems. However, that is not necessarily *sacrificial love*. The Walk to Emmaus program uses a retreat format to help develop leaders in local churches. It has put at its core the notion of *agape* love. Dr. MacArthur said that: "the word *agapē* means the love of the will, or the love of choice, not emotion." There are people involved in behind-the-scenes roles that are praying, cooking, cleaning, and distributing free items that are all designed to demonstrate what true servanthood is like. It is an interesting concept for leadership. More is said in the next section and again in Appendix G.

So, here's the short answer for now: we just don't see it as fulfilling to perform such service to people who don't seem to appreciate it. We're going to look at a lot of that as we look at the landscape before us. It is my desire for you to find ways to get over it and consider ways to change the system. We can't ever eliminate all of the apathy, etc., but going about the work we have to do in a better way can be very helpful.

In the end, being a disciple means being disciplined. Stay tuned for some possibilities.

We Are Called to Be Discerning

Sacrificial love is much of what we all should be about as Christians. There are some concerns we have in considering how we go about it. In the apostle Paul's letter to the Philippians, his opening in Chapter 1 includes this:

And this I pray, that your love may abound still more and more in real knowledge and all discernment, so that you may approve the things that are excellent, in order to be sincere and blameless until the day of Christ; having been filled with the fruit of righteousness which comes through Jesus Christ, to the glory and praise of God. (vv. 9-11)

That's sort of a mouthful, but there are some real kernels in it. He connects love with knowledge and discernment together. You will see the importance of this as we start considering solutions. The other thing that stands out to me is the *fruit of righteousness* we will get by being sincere. The basic point of this book is to learn how to be fruitful.

New Testament scholar and author of Bible commentaries, William Hendriksen (MacArthur 2018), wrote,

A person who possesses love but lacks discernment may reveal a great deal of eagerness and enthusiasm. He may donate to all kinds of causes. His motives may be worthy and his intentions honorable, yet he may be doing more harm than good.

We Are Called to Persevere

Here's a little story about what should happen when God does "speak" to us. The story is allegory, but the point is valid:

A man was sleeping one night in his cabin when suddenly his room filled with light, and God appeared. The Lord told the man he had worked for him and showed him a large rock in front of his cabin. The Lord explained that the man was to push against the rock with all his might...

So, this the man did, day after day. For many years, he toiled from sunup to sundown, his shoulders set squarely against the cold, massive surface of the unmoving rock, pushing with all his might! Each night, the man returned to sore and worn out, feeling that his whole day had been spent in vain.

Since the man was showing discouragement, the Adversary (Satan) decided to enter the picture by placing thoughts into the man's weary mind. (He will do it every time!) "You have been pushing against that rock for a long time and moved." Thus, he gave the man the impression that the task was impossible and that he was a failure.

These thoughts discouraged and disheartened the man. Satan said,

"Why kill yourself over this? Just put in your time, giving just the minimum effort, and that will be good enough." That's what the weary man planned to do, but decided to make it a matter of prayer and to take his troubled thoughts to the Lord.

"Lord," he said, "I have labored long and hard in Your service, putting all my strength to do that which you have asked. Yet, after all this time, I have not even budged that rock by half a millimeter. What is wrong? Why am I failing?"

The Lord responded compassionately, "My friend, when I asked you to serve Me, and you accepted, I told you that your task was to push against the rock with all of your strength, which you have done. Never once did I mention to you that I expected you to move it. Your task was to push. And now you come to Me with your strength spent, thinking that you have failed. But is that really so? Look at yourself. Your arms are strong and muscled, your back shiny and brown; Your hands are callused from constant pressure; your legs have become massive and hard. Through opposition you have grown much, and your abilities now surpass that which you used to have. True, you haven't moved the rock. But your calling was to be obedient and to push and to exercise your faith and trust in Mywisdom. That you have done, now I, my friend, will move the rock."

At times, when we hear a word from God, we tend to use our own intellect to decipher what He wants, when actually, what God wants is just simple obedience and faith in Him. By all means, exercise the faith that moves mountains, but know that it is still God who moves the mountains.

I've already said that I have not been very good at this, so you will have to realize it took me a long time to "get it." When I did, it was like a major rewind of my memory banks. I realized the truth of the saying that: "You have to live life forward, but you can only understand it in reverse." All of a sudden, what had seemed like coincidences made sense in the bigger scheme of things. The main one was *perseverance*. I've heard it said life is worthwhile if you stay. I remembered many occasions when I had persevered and was glad. Don't get me wrong; there are certainly times when you have to reconcile yourself to the fact that it's over.

We Are Called to Completion

This might better be called *restoration*. Candidates for ordination in the United Methodist tradition are asked if they are "going on toward perfection." Jesus was the only person who was *perfect*, but we are supposed to strive for it. We know one day, Jesus will return, and His rule will be eternal. Theologians may argue what that really means, but we do know something about what it means to live in a world broken by separation from God. By living a life of discipleship, we can help bring others into a life of God's truth.

What I am seeking to prepare the reader for is to help restore people's lives in a way they can know the truth of God. Many things break our lives; I don't have to go over a long list. However, nothing breaks like separation from God. Blaise Pascal (Pascal 1669) has been credited with saying we have a God-shaped hole in our hearts that only God can fill. I believe that St. Augustine (St. Augustine, Goodreads 2018) said our soul is restless until it finds rest in God. It seems that one of the greatest things we can do as a disciple is to help people to find that rest. Further, I hope that you will find this book helpful in showing how to model the things Jesus did. Hopefully, we can help people find ways to live a productive life and grow the Kingdom of God.

Other Aspects of Our Call

Living up to the previous components of our call from God is not something we should take lightly, and they are not easy to do. We must stay in prayer and look to the Holy Spirit to guide us and support us in this endeavor. There are other aspects which will become apparent as you read on. Some of these are:

- To be in the world but not of the world – 1 John 2:15-16
- To be humble – Psalm 25:9
- To be in fellowship with one another – 1 John 1:6-7
- To create relationships wherever possible – 2 Corinthians 5:18

- To exhibit *holiness* as being set aside for God's work - 1 Thessalonians 4:7
- To be a part of the Body of Christ - 1 Corinthians 12:12-27
- To be a leader in the church or a faithful follower – 1 Corinthians 12:27-28
- To realize that, in the end, we are to be servants of Christ- Ephesians 6:5b-6

Chapter questions:

Have you sensed a call from God? If so, what was it like? How did you respond?

Have you taken a Spiritual gifts assessment? If you did, how did it change your life?

Why do you think that *perseverance* might be so important? Do you have trouble seeing things through to the end?

Can you think of any other aspects of a *call* than the ones lifted up in this chapter?

The rest of Part I will add to the preparation you need to take on this important and somewhat daunting task. It gets a little strong at times, but all of this is important in helping overcome a mindset holding back real progress in restoring dignity.

CHAPTER 2

REAL PROFIT: A MANDATE FOR RESULTS

How do we view profit?

To most people, the word profit has to do with a business transaction. The motto of a former hardware wholesaler has always intrigued me. It said, "Profit is not a four-letter word." There are many people who don't think profit has a place in a society that values people. When I was in business in Mississippi, I heard the results of a survey done by the Mississippi Dept. of Economic Development involving high school students. They were asked what they believed the average amount of profit businesses made was. The answer was 75%. The next question was: how much profit do you think they should make? The answer was ZERO. The real number at the time was something less than 5%, on average.

Before you start getting irritated and try to tell me I must be smoking something funny, let me clarify the number. I am not naïve. I know corporations give dividends to stockholders and pay accountants large sums to avoid paying taxes. No doubt, games are played with earnings in order to make the picture be whatever they want it to be. I never worked for a corporation (except my own) that didn't figure out a way to make monthly earnings look better than they really were. So, think about it: why would a publicly traded corporation or even a closely held one want to portray losses as gains? It's in order to make their situation look better than it really is. Obvious answer, right? So why would they want to portray gains as losses to avoid paying taxes? It gets a little complicated here. There are obvious ways that accountants can lessen the impact of taxes that are legal and legitimate (so that investors would understand it). As a business broker, I routinely recast the financials of my clients in order to give a more accurate picture of the income available to a new owner. This could be anything from expenses in payment for personal items to travel that might be a bit unnecessary. Taxes have been avoided on those items, but nothing "funny" was going on.

Donald Trump, in his run for the U. S. presidency was badgered repeatedly for not releasing his tax returns. His opposition blasted him for it and claimed there were some nefarious things going on he didn't want to expose. It didn't help for him to say his attorney advised him not to release them due to him being under an audit from the IRS. Amazingly, his 1995 return was "mailed" to the New York Times, and it showed he had almost a $1 billion loss. The benefit to Trump was that he could use that loss to offset any tax liability from subsequent gains. The reason the Trump campaign gave for the gigantic loss was a downturn in the areas where he was heavily invested. I'm pretty sure that Trump didn't seek to lose all that money. Some of it may have been a "paper loss." In other words, it was a loss in value (on paper) and not actual dollars. What Trump did with his taxes was to take advantage of tax law that enabled him to do it. I haven't heard a credible source say that it was illegal.

What might have been the benefit of offsetting gains with losses spread over a large number of years? To Trump, it meant he wasn't punished by paying taxes on money he had gained so that his business could continue. For his suppliers, employees, and other businesses who benefited from the "trickle-down" effect, it meant they would survive and grow from income and investments not taken away in taxes.

For those people who say, "You didn't build that," no explanation like the one I just provided will make any difference. To them, whatever a business makes should go to the government anyway. It doesn't matter that the government does a very poor job of using the money they get. A lot of this money may go to worthwhile projects, but much of it goes to projects the government isn't capable of managing wisely. The most notable of late was for a company named Solyndra that manufactured solar panels. The company hired a bunch of people but never produced anything. The loss to taxpayers was about $500 million! Safety, roads, education (questionable), and interstate affairs should be the purview of the federal government. Safety covers a lot of areas, such as police, military, natural disasters, and the like. However, the federal government is involved in a lot more than just these categories. For example, they are the largest landowners on the planet. National Forests and other set-aside property take property off the tax rolls and inhibit individuals and businesses from taking advantage of the property for money-making purposes. Please don't think that I am anti-environment, but the Environmental Protection Agency (EPA) does a lot of damage from bad decisions and removes capital from the economy with Draconian measures and fees/penalties.

What about non-profits?

If profit is so bad, then non-profits should be the best organizations around, right? Non-profit businesses haven't normally gotten the same kind of scrutiny, but this has changed in the past few years. When the Susan G. Komen Foundation got a lot of attention over their Planned Parenthood support, the salaries of their CEO and of several other non-profits were brought to the public's attention. To some degree, the problems in Haiti show what happens when human nature overtakes the desire to "do the right thing." Before the earthquake in 2010, there were over 10,000 Non-Governmental Organizations (NGOs) at work in Haiti. Very little was being done to change the deplorable conditions of the average citizen of that country. I was the mission chair at Delmar Baptist Church in St. Louis at the time. Delmar (now known as Dayspring) was supporting a missionary in northern Haiti, so I was paying close attention to what was happening there in order to report to the congregation. I came across an article taking NGOs to task for their ineffective efforts in Haiti. Most of those who were supposed to be recipients of the aid being sent to the country did not see much in the way of any benefit of the aid. Samaritan's Purse, the organization created by Franklin Graham, was one of only three that were actually doing anything significant. The rest were living in good quarters and driving big cars rather than providing much aid to the needy.

In his first book, *Toxic Charity* (Lupton 2011, 5-6), Robert Lupton indicts religious mission trip efforts. There are estimates (probably higher now) that the "industry" consumes between $2.5 and 5.0 billion annually with very little to show for it. When I was at Delmar, I went on one of these mission trips the church, along with several others, had been supporting for over 15 years. I was obliged to go because of my position, but my heart wasn't in it. It cost me $600 for travel, and none of it went for any of the projects we were working on. Of course, food and lodging establishments benefited from some of my expenditures, and the building supply company got a lot of the funds paid for by Delmar's and the other churches' contributions. The sad part is that after 15 years and all the work that had been done, no one there was taking the initiative to try to work themselves out of the business of perpetuating dependency. In fact, two more organizations moved in to do the same thing the church groups had been doing. The "killer" for me was when the town refused to participate in the rehabbing of a gymnasium for youth activities. Instead, they let the "sweat equity" and financial contributions from the mission teams help them to get a grant from the state Department of Education to complete the job! To my way of thinking, they could have at least helped do some of the work.

I got convicted to do this work a different way on a trip to southeastern Tennessee. This was year-round and included Vacation Bible School in the summer months as well as building/rehabbing houses all year. Volunteers paid for their room and board and provided funds for the housing efforts. They worked side-by-side with the homeowners or family members. While this project did not provide jobs directly, the population of the area stabilized and began to grow, thus enticing businesses to locate in the area. In turn, small businesses sprang up to support the larger businesses and the new residents.

Lupton also points out that almost 90% of Americans are involved in some sort of charitable effort. However, without accountability, these efforts are generally missing the mark. In his latest book, Charity Detox (Lupton 2015, 67-88), Lupton cites many organizations that have changed their focus to see to it that they are accountable for what they do. I'll have a lot more to say about this later.

God and profit

Lost yet? Well, let me try to make a big point here: business people are generally like all Americans who receive a paycheck. Yeah, right, you say. So, hear me out. There are many people who skirt the system on both sides of the issue. Fudging on taxes is a great American activity. Given the way the Internal Revenue Service (IRS) operates, it is easy to sympathize with those of us who appear to be in the same boat. I think what makes the statement implausible is that independent business people seem to be considered the same as corporations. Independents don't play games with their income because they can't afford to. Believe me, I hate having to pay unemployment taxes when I have seldom laid anyone off. I never closed a business without helping employees find a job – sometimes better than the one they had with me. As an owner, I was required to pay unemployment taxes on my wife and me even though owners are not allowed to collect it. Look, I understand that people have gamed the system and we all have to pay the price, but I am getting way ahead of myself in how profit really works.

Let's look at some definitions of the word:

Profit – noun - a: pecuniary gain resulting from the employment of capital in any transaction. b: returns, proceeds, or revenue, as from property or investments. c: the monetary surplus left to a producer or employer after deducting wages, rent, cost of raw materials, etc. d: advantage; benefit; gain.

Profit – verb- a: to gain an advantage or benefit b: to make progress

Profit – synonyms – a: return b: good, welfare, advancement, improvement

Do you see instances not exclusively related to business in these definitions? Specifically, capital, transactions, investments, advantage, surplus, benefit, gain, and all the synonyms listed are words that certainly apply to how we interact with people in non-business settings.

22

The disconnect comes between for-profit and non-profit organizations.

Here, I want to make a departure into the real philosophy of business and profit. The Bible is not afraid to address profit as an important part of life. That's not because God wants your money The church may, but God wants your heart. I once said something to that effect to a church leader during a stewardship campaign. He didn't know how to respond. I'm pretty sure it was because he didn't get my point. Maybe he didn't expect that sort of response. Why do churches have stewardship campaigns anyway? We're giving back to God, right? Of course, we are, but what is God going to do with our money? If you believe that God has any power at all, you have to believe God could create money for anything He wants. Didn't He make gold, silver, platinum, and everything else? Well, why does He want us to give it back to Him if he doesn't need it? Here's what Jesus had to say about it: where your treasure is, there will your heart be also. If the treasure that fills your heart is monetary wealth, you may not have room for God. He wants you to give it up so He can fill your heart with love unimaginable. God loves the church; He has chosen it as the way people live out the calling He places on our lives. Churches do need money to operate, and we should clearly support that. However, a pastor friend of mine once told me he was pessimistic about the future of the church, in part because of the cost of maintenance of the facilities. Sadly, I see many churches trying to keep a building program going, mainly, it seems, because it makes the church look like it is successful. Some are, but one does have to consider if the funds could be put to better use. It is this inward focus that, in some ways, comes from the view of expenditures made to mission activities. I have already expressed the case for much of the money spent in that endeavor. However, spending money on church facilities, staff, and programs only intended for that church's members is not the only alternative and certainly not the best one.

Money is not the only thing that captures people's hearts rather than letting God have them. Donald McCullough, in *Waking from the American Dream* (McCullough 1988, 71-84), points to power and religion as other gods standing in the way of hearts being given to God. It's clear both power and religion involve money in many, many ways. Money is power, and it can mean prestige as well. It is attractive and alluring. This is not because of its appearance, for sure. It is what money can buy that has these characteristics. People who have money may have power, although some don't use it. However, if you know much about religion, you know money can be a problem there as well. It's amazing to me what people will give money for in churches. It's not always about power in these cases. Perhaps you have heard it said if you give more, God will bless you more. Whoa! Where did that come from? Debatable for sure, but why is it then people give what they do? Jesus said you should give privately, but many people want others to know how much they give. Maybe the rationale is that God knows anyway, but people will know what a good person they are if they give lots publicly. Buildings, plaques, monuments, and even trees become "evidence" of the goodness of people's hearts because of what they gave. He goes on to say if you get your reward in this life, you won't get any later on – in eternity. I'm not fooling myself about people's motivations; I've lived on this planet for a long time. I have lived in many places and been a member of many churches. Trust me; that can make you cynical.

You may be familiar with the story where Jesus told his followers that the widow who gave a very small amount actually gave more because it was all she had (Lk. 21:1-4). He also told rich people they needed to sell what they had and give it to the poor (Mt. 19:16-22). He didn't get any takers we know of. Jesus lost it at the temple over moneychangers, etc., taking advantage of well-meaning worshippers (Mt. 21:12-13). After His death and resurrection, Ananias and Sapphira both dropped dead after being exposed for lying about making good on their promise to give God what they had gotten from a property sale (Acts 5:1-11).

Here are several passages (with some comments) from the Bible that address how we are to view profit:

Leviticus 25 36 – "Do not take any interest or any profit from them, but fear your God, so that they may continue to live among you." Meant to keep from taking advantage of the poor. John Wesley said this doesn't apply to modern business situations at legal rates of interest. (Proverbs 28:8)

Proverbs 14:23 – "All hard work brings a profit, but mere talk only to poverty."

Proverbs 21:5 "The plans of the diligent lead to profit as surely as haste leads to poverty."

Ecclesiastes 6:11: "The more the words, the less the meaning, and how does that profit anyone?"

Isaiah 23:18: "Yet her profit and her earnings will be set apart for the LORD, they will not be stored up or hoarded. Her profits will go to those who live before the LORD, for abundant food and fine clothes." Referring to Tyre.

Isaiah 44:10: "Who shapes a god and casts an idol, which can profit nothing?"

2 Corinthians 2:17: "Unlike so many, we do not peddle the word of God for profit. On the contrary, in Christ, we speak before God with sincerity, as those sent from God."

Mark 8:36: "For what shall it profit a man, if he shall gain the whole world, and lose his own soul?"

Some of this is about money, but much of it is just about what happens as a result of human activity. It is pretty well summed up in Mark 8:36. As David McCullough (McCullough 1988, 71-84) points out, this is about taking the place of God. Gain or profit comes at a cost. Not all activities produce profit. Yeah, I know that we're not always responsible for the outcome, but we are responsible for being faithful to your calling. There is profit in that.

If you haven't taken a Spiritual gifts assessment, do it as soon as possible! For me, it was the most liberating thing I could have done. Being a business person, I was naturally drawn to committees that related to business-type activities: trustees, finance, stewardship, and personnel. I quickly found out that what I knew about business wasn't welcomed by most church folks. For-profit and not-for-profit enterprises operate very differently when it comes to managing money. One is concerned about the bottom line, and the other is focused on having enough money to do what they have budgeted for. In the latter case, not having enough revenue to meet all budgeted items means sitting down and redistributing what you have or making a last-minute appeal to cover the shortfall. In the former, it is about making every effort to reach the revenue and profit goals. You may not see the point, but please stay with me.

When I took the (Spiritual gifts) assessment, I learned a lot about myself. All of the business-related experiences I brought into my church "work" eventually helped me understand these things make the main job of the church possible: making disciples for Jesus Christ.

I am a business consultant, but mainly a consultant. Those skills have prepared me to help people understand the role money and profit play in being faithful followers of Christ. Hopefully you will come to see business people need to be able to give their hearts to God as we all do. In *The Gospel for the Person Who Has Everything* (Willimon 1978), Will Willimon suggests an approach that involves couching the project or whatever in some sort of interesting manner. This could be something like making the project seem "sexy." It might also be something that pulls at the heartstrings. It is very indirect in that it doesn't have the overtones of a religious experience attached to it. I don't know - I have the greatest respect for him, but I suppose I just prefer a less nuanced method.

One of the best books I have read on the subject is *Church on Sunday, Work on Monday* (Nash 2001, xxi-xxxi). The authors point out that while there is a strong interest in *spirituality*, this has not done anything to bridge the gap between clergy and businesspeople. It's not hard to figure out even regular churchgoers spend the vast majority of their time away from the church. Those who are involved in several activities at the church still only spend a few additional hours involved with matters relating to the church. This means that, regardless of how seriously you take your religious faith, you are far more influenced by the secular world than the spiritual one.

Luke 16: As a Basis

I have recently founded an organization under the corporate name Luke 16 Corp. The inspiration for this was the parable in the New Testament book of Luke. This parable has various names, some of them more derogatory than others. Most refer to it as *The Shrewd Manager* (all passages come from *The Message*):

Jesus said to his disciples, "There was once a rich man who had a manager. He got reports that the manager had been taking advantage of his position by running up huge personal expenses. So, he called him in and said, 'What's this I hear about you? You're fired. And I want a complete audit of your books.'" The manager said to himself, 'What am I going to do? I've lost my job as manager. I'm not strong enough for a laboring job, and I'm too proud to beg. . .Ah, I've got a plan. Here's what I'll do . . . then when I'm turned out into the street, people will take me into their houses.' "Then he went at it. One after another, he called in the people who were in debt to his master. He said to the first, 'How much do you owe my master?'" He replied, 'A hundred jugs of olive oil.' "The manager said, 'Here, take your bill, sit down here - quick now - write fifty.'" To the next, he said, 'And you, what do you owe?' "He answered, 'A hundred sacks of wheat.'" He said, 'Take your bill, write in eighty.' "Now, here's a surprise: The master praised the crooked manager! And why? Because he knew how to look after himself. Streetwise people are smarter in this regard than law-abiding citizens. They are on constant alert, looking for angles, surviving by their wits. I want you to be smart in the same way - but for what is right - using every adversity to stimulate you to creative survival, to concentrate your attention on the bare essentials, so you'll live, really live, and not complacently just get by on good behavior." (vv.1-9)

This is a head-scratcher for most people. It's important to focus on what appears to be the point Jesus wants to make: Use your wits and turn your difficulties into opportunities. Live so that you are fully alive and not just avoiding error. It's been appropriately said, "If you aren't making mistakes, you aren't doing anything." We are to be focused on what is important. Other translations, such as the English Standard Version, put it this way: "And I tell you, make friends for yourselves by means of unrighteous wealth so that when it fails, they will welcome you into eternal dwellings." John MacArthur (MacArthur 1997, 1547) describes this as investing in the Kingdom gospel in order to bring sinners to salvation. Those sinners will be waiting to welcome you if you do that. Other versions say something very close to that. No matter whose version you choose, it is still a bit confusing.

So, let me share how I see this. After all, choosing to name my ministry after this chapter of the Bible is a little unusual. I actually got interested in it when I was in a Sunday school class that was considering this parable. The author made the point that the manager may have marked down the debt because it was what his commission would have been on the transaction. I have actually found another writer who postulated that, and it does put a different light on the matter.

Bibleway Commentaries offers this:

I favor the commission view because I find it hardly credible for the master to commend a steward who has just cheated him. If the reductions are dishonest price cuts, they constitute further injustice against the master beyond the steward's earlier squandering. If so, the master now has two charges against the steward: ineptitude followed by dishonesty. The traditional view hardly allows the steward to gain credibility and respect. Another problem is that Jesus himself praises the steward's actions in his subsequent remarks. Would he really commend such immoral behavior?

It is better to see that the previously dishonest steward learns something by his failure and comes up with a generous solution, one that can be commended. In my view, the master commends his formerly dishonest steward for a shrewd solution. The steward has sacrificed what he could have taken now and has given it to others so that he can receive gain later. The implicit moral about perspective in the use of resources is exactly the application Jesus makes in verse 9.

Jesus' applications extend in various directions. First, he notes that people of the world are more shrewd than the people of the light (the disciples) are. People of this world think about how they use their resources. Even if they misuse them, they still give it thought. They think about the long-term benefits of what they acquire. Disciples should apply themselves to honor and serve God by their use of resources. They should think through their actions, both short and long-term.

If you think about it, it makes sense that marking down the debt in the amount of the commission owed was the fair thing to do in that case. Everyone wins in this case, albeit the manager only benefits in the long run. Well, I believe we should consider the practical advice inherent in the parable. Wealth is considered "unrighteous." It only gets that way by how it is used when in the hands of a human. This makes the activity of handling money/wealth into a way of building the Kingdom. We try that when we build church buildings, go on mission trips, hand money to beggars, and many other ways. Jesus is not impressed by this. Many times, we do these things to impress the world. The real point of this book and the Luke 16 ministry is to help explore ways to use wealth to truly build the Kingdom.

> Jesus went on to make these comments: If you're honest in small things, you'll be honest in big things; If you're a crook in small things, you'll be a crook in big things. If you're not honest in small jobs, who will put you in charge of the store? No worker can serve two bosses: He'll either hate the first or love the second. Or adore the first and despise the second. You can't serve both God and the Bank. (vv. 10-13)

This portion deals with honesty and priorities. Both are very true and characterized human behavior. The manager may have been the crook; certainly, people who get reimbursement for personal expenses "pad" them on occasion. It may seem like an overkill to take such strident measures to deal with something that is usually not a major offense. So maybe it wasn't minor; perhaps it rose to the level of embezzling. We don't know, but the point Jesus made here suggests that proportionality doesn't come into play in such matters. Think about it: unless someone steals something as minor as a pencil, it doesn't make any difference if you are expecting to be able to trust them. What if it is time? In other words, sneaking in late or leaving without "clocking out" is stealing just as sure as taking some material thing. People avoid being noticed when they slip out so they don't have to have their pay reduced. What might that person do when the amount of the theft is larger? The ways this is done are legion. I wouldn't want to give anyone any ideas, so I'll avoid more examples at this point. The real point is we don't want to do this with God. If your priority of making money exceeds your desire to be honest and you don't believe God cares, all bets may be off.

> When the Pharisees, a money-obsessed bunch, heard him say these things, they rolled their eyes, dismissing him

as hopelessly out of touch. So, Jesus spoke to them: "You are masters at making yourselves look good in front of others, but God knows what's behind the appearance. What society sees and calls monumental, God sees through and calls monstrous." (vv. 14-15)

So much for trying to disguise who you are. When society chooses to value the monetary success of people, God gets overlooked. We really need to rethink how we value money and everything else that keeps us from putting God first. The famous story that follows puts wealth into perspective like no other passage, I believe:

"There once was a rich man, expensively dressed in the latest fashions, wasting his days in conspicuous consumption. A poor man named Lazarus, covered with sores, had been dumped on his doorstep. All he lived for was to get a meal from scraps off the rich man's table. His best friends were the dogs who came and licked his sores." Then he died, this poor man, and was taken up by the angels to the lap of Abraham. The rich man also died and was buried. In hell and in torment, he looked up and saw Abraham in the distance and Lazarus in his lap. He called out, 'Father Abraham, mercy! Have mercy! Send Lazarus to dip his finger in water to cool my tongue. I'm in agony in this fire.' "But Abraham said, 'Child, remember that in your lifetime you got the good things and Lazarus the bad things. It's not like that here. Here, he's consoled, and you're tormented. Besides, in all these matters there is a huge chasm set between us so that no one can go from us to you even if he wanted to, nor can anyone cross over from you to us.' "The rich man said, 'Then let me ask you, Father: Send him to the house of my father where I have five brothers, so he can tell them the score and warn them so they won't end up here in this place of torment.'" Abraham answered, 'They have Moses and the Prophets to tell them the score. Let them listen to them.' "'I know, Father Abraham,' he said, 'but they're not listening. If someone came back to them from the dead, they would change their ways.'" Abraham replied, 'If they won't listen to Moses and the Prophets, they're not going to be convinced by someone who rises from the dead.'" (vv. 19-31)

This is a pretty sad reality – Jesus is saying there's no reason to tell the brothers. After all, they didn't pay attention to what was already available to them. They surely would have heard this message from the way Jesus tells this story. It suggests to us in our current place, in the bigger scheme of things, we may be doomed to the same fate. Jesus is even suggesting they don't believe Him, so it would be useless to send someone less than He.

This Is Personal

With every bone in my body, I believe Jesus was the only perfect human being who ever lived. In that role, He was the perfect model for how we are supposed to live. There are, of course, people who don't believe Jesus is God who do believe Him to be a "good man." He was asked by the rich young man mentioned above what good thing he needed to do to have eternal life. (Mt. 19:16). Apparently, Jesus understood what the man was asking and asked him: "Why do you ask me about what is good? There is only one who is good. If you would enter life, keep the commandments." (v. 17). The man must have gotten the point and asked "which ones?" (v. 18). However, the point is, in order to truly be a follower of Jesus, we need to model the behavior we see in His life. When He was asked which commandment was the greatest (Mt. 22:36-38), He said it was to love God with all your heart and with all your soul and with all your mind. Then He said the second one was like the first: love your neighbor as yourself (v.39). Going back to the matter of treasure, this is the point about what has our heart.

DO PEOPLE REALLY GIVE MUCH THOUGHT TO THEIR NEIGHBORS? WITHOUT A CLEAR INSTRUCTION TO LOVE OUR NEIGHBOR, THERE'S A GOOD CHANCE WE WOULDN'T DO IT. HECK, MANY OF US DON'T EVEN KNOW OUR NEIGHBORS.

We are a pretty selfish bunch, we humans. Money gets blamed for it, but I have heard it suggested one of the reasons people think ill of others who have money is they don't trust themselves. In other words, they feel like having money corrupts a person. If you have seen enough examples of people who are rich and corrupt, you can get pretty jaundiced. If they have become corrupted by having it, others who have it would probably get corrupted, too. Basically, it doesn't take money to corrupt people; they can be corrupted in other ways. I will admit that money seems to be a tipping point many times. Marriages that are in trouble can go the way of greed. Reasons seem to come from every direction to justify some action if there is a concern about losing something. Some examples are a marriage that is going to mean loss of custody of children or a person in a position of power or prestige faced with losing it. It's amazing what a possible insurance payout will do to a troubled relationship. If you don't think so, spend some time watching episodes of NBC's Dateline or CBS's 48 Hours, just to name a couple. It is not a long journey from rationalization to blame in many cases. If you can make the other person the source of your problems, you can maybe make yourself (or Satan can) believe extreme methods are justified.

Jealousy is a very insidious, dangerous trap many get sucked into. While the examples may be legion, mostly jealousy leads to covetousness. I believe it all can be traced back to greed. We want more, or we want what someone else has (actually coveting). So, if you look at the nature of many very wealthy people, you can see money many times is not the focus of their "greed." It is usually more about what money can do for them. As mentioned earlier, it does bring power in many cases. Napoleon Hill wrote in *Think and Grow Rich* (Hill 1937, 240) that for some, getting money is like a sexual experience. In other words, it's the process and the conquest, not the power or the money. That has a lot of logic, given that the super-rich seem to continually make dumb decisions in trying to move beyond what made them successful in the first place.

The only reason for discussing this matter now is to begin to move toward a more in-depth consideration of what profit is and what it is not. I have shown that many of the words used to define profit don't have to do with money (or at least not exclusively). So, what I am saying is almost every endeavor is designed to provide a profit or gain of some sort. If not, a person would have to be a masochist to take on such a fool's errand. Here's a new saying: If you plan to fail, you'll probably succeed. Twisted logic for sure, so I'm not sure anyone does that. For argument's sake, let's assume profit or gain is indeed the goal of every endeavor undertaken.

Vision Is Critical

With that, we should consider what it means to succeed and have a profit or a gain. Obviously, every situation will be different to some degree, but the amount of profit is less important at this point than understanding what it is. Laurence Peter (Peter 1969) once said, if you don't know where you're going, how do you know when you get there? Let me add that you should be able to understand what it means to have achieved a profit. Let me give an example. Say you are operating a food pantry. What would a profit look like? Good question, huh? Food pantries are non-profit enterprises. So, you would naturally say there is no profit. Think about it, if that is the case, how do you know when you have succeeded? A logical guess would be you have worked yourself out of business. Aha! Weren't expecting that were you? What would it mean if you no longer had clients (or whatever you call the people you are serving)? Most people would say you had failed. How can that be? Well, it could be these people have gone somewhere else. That's not good either because they have been dealt a bad hand. The goal of the food pantry perhaps should be to be out of business because all the people they were serving had "graduated." The gain or profit would be to have fewer people to serve. Is that really doing a service to the people though? It is if the people formerly served have become self-sufficient. The other benefit is the cost of putting on the pantry can now be diverted into something else that needs that support. However, this is certainly not the most practical outcome nor is it not completely desirable. After all, there are people who can only be served by food pantries. I would recommend reading about what Robert Ludlum has done as he relates it in *Toxic Charity*.

Would it be realistic for a food pantry to go out of business because it did its job well? I can't conceive of that ever happening, given the way people feel about them. However, it is not going to ever happen for sure unless people make a mental shift in how they view the concept. A missionary who operates a food pantry I was involved in a few years ago told me a story. One day when they were serving their clients, a church member commented on the fact that they only had 75 families there that day. Normally, there were in the neighborhood of 150 families in attendance. Without making a judgment, I would like to state emphatically it may be a good thing for there to be fewer families than "usual." Getting back to 150 families may mean new clients are being served. That's good news for people who need it and haven't been served, but it may be a sign excess capacity has attracted people who had been knocked off the list elsewhere. It's hard not to be judgmental when speaking of such situations, but there are many who have extensive experience serving the poor who have strong feelings about how this is being done. The problem is these programs tend not to work themselves out of business. Some hang on for years after their usefulness has expired.

It is my contention the problem lies in what I wrote of earlier: there is no plan to measure results. Profit in a food pantry should mean people have graduated from the program. People do, for sure, but most of the time, it is because they have the drive to make better lives for themselves. Many programs have a means to connect clients with job opportunities, but they tend to miss the mark on a broad scale. Much hesitancy crops up when deciding how to help people beyond just providing them with some food. It is certainly a bit obtuse to consider profit as being a reduction in clients served. OK, but when you use synonyms like gain, return, benefit, and good, it is easier to see that less is more in such cases.

A lot of why I am writing this book is to provide as much guidance as I can in order to educate those who are embarking on a new venture or trying to get a mulligan (a golfing term meaning a "do-over") for an existing one. My point is, as I have been toying with, every endeavor should have a point where they recognize a desirable outcome or realize they missed the mark and move on. You can only do this if you have planned enough to know what it should look like.

Every venture, for-profit or not-for-profit, needs a plan. That plan for a not-for-profit needs to be more than how funds are going to be spent. If it is not a project that is based on a finite amount from a grant or the like, it is going to need to determine where the funds are coming from to complete and/or sustain it. I have seen too many worthwhile projects fail to get sufficient funding because they haven't made the sale in terms of outcomes. With the climate today very different from times past, funds just aren't lying around waiting to be snapped up.

The development director for a mainline Christian denomination once told me that he had an interesting discovery when he took that job. He had done the same thing (essentially fundraising) for another denomination prior to taking his current one. He noticed that many of the donors to his current denomination were not nearly as large as his previous one. Now, one might think that the reason was obvious: it was the reason that it had turned out that way. Not so, at least according to him. He said that it was that the donors believed in both of the denominations; it was just that they didn't see his current employer doing enough to deserve more. So, does this not sound like the parable of the talents? I remember hearing Walt Disney say that it doesn't matter what you have: it's "what you do with what you got." The consideration of this parable and the story of the donors spawns several thoughts. First, we may not get what we think we deserve. Second, what we do about it is really what matters. Third, we may think that what we get is unfair, but we weren't the one(s) who made that decision. You can't please everyone, but you can do what is right. In the end, there is only one you answer to: the holy God.

Let me reiterate:

1. All projects, regardless of their purpose, need to ensure that they have a plan that takes into consideration how it can be sustained until that purpose is realized.

2. In order to succeed, you have to first define what success will look like. You have to recognize that success might end up being something different, but you can hopefully determine that as you review and evaluate what you are doing.

3. It is critical to stay with your plan until you have achieved your purpose. Changes are OK, but giving up before you see the process through is not.

4. Review and evaluation are absolutely necessary to make sure you are on track. It is a sad thing to get too far down the road

before recognizing that change is absolutely required.

5. Play the hand you are dealt. Folding should only come when all is lost.

6. Seek the help of those who can assist you make the best decisions.

Chapter questions:

- The first section asks, "How do we view profit?" Do you agree?

- Do you think that non-profits need profit (gain or whatever)?

- A lot was shared about what the Bible says about *profit*. Is this an accurate portrayal of what God has to say about it?

- Do you consider yourself to be a *visionary*? Any project will be difficult to achieve without it.

CHAPTER 3

ACCOUNTABILITY

One of the problems I have always had with nonprofits in general and Christian groups in particular is a lack of accountability. We look at Social Entrepreneurship later, but a business approach to projects includes considering results. The title of Robert Lupton's second book, *Charity Detox* (Lupton 2015), has as its subtitle, *What Charity Would Look Like If We Cared About Results.* His first book, *Toxic Charity* (Lupton 2011), drew me in with the notion of changing how we went about doing charitable deeds. *Detox* cemented it with examples of how businesspeople were changing the process with a results-oriented approach.

Maybe there is a lack of understanding about what *accountability* means in the world of charity. Perhaps it would be good to understand charity before we do that. One definition is the voluntary giving of help, typically in the form of money, to those in need. Some charity organizations mainly receive cash donations to fund their efforts. Occasionally, donations of property of some form are accepted and then sold for cash if they can't be used in the operation of the charity. Most of the time, there isn't much scrutiny done on the organizations unless there is some reason to be concerned. The IRS is getting better at cracking down on some of the fraudulent players, but there isn't as much consideration of how much of the money goes to its intended purpose. When a disaster of some sort occurs, scams are rampant because people can only send cash donations unless there is a need for food, clothing, and other essentials.

What It Means to Be Accountable

The common definition of accountability begins with the first part of the word: account. The way we think of an *account* is generally in a business setting, like a *checking account*. In this case, the meanings are mostly nouns as in bank accounts, business accounts, and now, a *Twitter account*, etc. However, an account as an oral or written description of a particular event or situation narrative is also a noun. Another more important way to describe it is an explanatory statement of conduct as to a superior. Jesus did speak to us about it in Matthew 12:36: "I tell you, on the day of judgment, people will give *account* for every careless word they speak." This should let you know how seriously He took responsibility. Commentaries soften this somewhat by letting us know that this has to do with infractions against God's holiness. In Luke 16:2, the story of the shrewd manager tells us he was "held to account" for what were reportedly running up huge personal expenses. Without getting too far afield on this, the point is that we can understand that God cares about our responsibility. Anyway, there are several instances where an *account* is used to point out that *accountability* should be a part of all that we are – especially when it comes to following the call God has placed on our hearts.

The difficulty that folks like me have encountered comes from trying to take the approach of accountability with people who have been involved with some sort of charitable endeavor.

DEEP IN THEIR COLLECTIVE PSYCHES IS THE NOTION THAT DOING FOR PEOPLE BY GIVING THEM SOMETHING IS ALL THAT WE ARE CALLED TO DO. IT IS NOT EASY TO GET THEM TO CHANGE THEIR MINDSET BECAUSE IT IS SO DEEPLY INGRAINED.

We Christians heard the message where Jesus told us to feed the hungry, clothe the naked, and care for the widows and orphans. Jesus even said that when we "did it to one of the least of these (we) did it to (Him)" (Matt. 25:40). There is nothing wrong with living up to that message; there are certainly many people in our world that need help. Jesus went on to say that if we don't do these things, we "will go away into eternal punishment" (v.46). The part that we miss is the message that He left, as recorded in Matthew 28:19-20. That is the one about going forth into all the world and making disciples. It has always seemed to me that while we should care about the lifespan and comfort of others, we should care much more about them meeting the living God through Jesus Christ. Rick Warren, in *A Purpose-Driven Life* (Warren 2002, 41-46), reminds us that God doesn't care about our comfort; he cares about our character.

From what I understand about Jesus' ministry, He was constantly followed around by people. Some of them wanted healing; the sincere ones wanted the "living water" and the "bread of life". Of course, there were the Pharisees that wanted to get some "dirt" on Him. So, why did Jesus feed the 5,000 (plus women and children) and 4,000 on another occasion and stop there? God fed the Israelites in the wilderness after they left Egypt and then gave them some meat when they complained. Of course, it was God's plan, and He was delivering them in order to further His plan. Jesus had a plan, too.

From what I can determine, Jesus' plan was to "show us the way." He did that with word and deed. His miracles were to show His authority. Who wants to follow someone who can do a few tricks? Many of the people who witnessed what He did were not clued into the meaning. In fact, His disciples didn't understand a lot of what it was all about until after the Resurrection. We should be thankful that the whole story was spelled out for us in the Bible. God, throughout the entire Scripture, held His people accountable. God made covenants with them and pledged to keep His part of them. Over and over again, the Israelites broke the covenants by not keeping their end of the bargain. God is really patient.

Free Will and Accountability

Free will is an interesting thing. People sometimes wonder why God would give us such amazing latitude. Most of us screw up at some point. School counselors who know about such things refer to it as sewing our wild oats. They say that almost everyone does it at some point – we just don't all do it at the same point in our lives. Some of us get over it quickly; others of us seem to get stuck in it and just get lost. It doesn't mean we necessarily become bad; it just means we lose sight of what we are supposed to be about for the time we are on earth.

In Chapter 1, I mentioned that Blaise Pascal (Pascal 1669) has been credited with the notion of a "God-shaped hole" in our hearts that only God can fill. This suggests that this is the condition we find ourselves in when we have strayed away from God. A lot of what makes us restless is that we are here for a purpose. It is a lot easier to be accountable in the tasks that we have before us if we are functioning in the arena of our spiritual gifts. We may think that we are doing what our talents enable us to do, but talents are different from spiritual gifts. A Spiritual Gifts Assessment can be very helpful in getting you directed. This should be followed up with a plan to learn how to live into your calling. At this point, we are still preparing for the journey, so you will hopefully excuse me for repeating this.

So, bringing this back to the point at hand, it turns out that free will is like most things considered to be free. It can be costly if you use your free will in ways that lead you away from God. Dietrich Bonhoeffer (Caffeinated Thoughts 2010) used "Cheap Grace" to describe how we degrade God's grace when we don't consider what the cost really is. So, to put it another way, grace is free, but it is not cheap. By sacrificing His Son, Jesus Christ, God showed what it was worth for Him to free us from the bondage of sin and death. The free will part of it is that we can choose whether to accept it or not. The obvious response to this good news is: who would not want it? As obvious as it might be to some, it is amazing that many, many people either don't accept it at all or play games with themselves, trying to minimize their responsibility in the matter. We are held accountable for what we are told to do in response to this amazing gift.

Ignoring the Problem Is Not an Option (it never is)

There must be a lot of the perception that we can ignore situations to the point that they don't exist. I wonder who sold them on that baloney. If you have invested enough in this book to get to this point, you surely know that to not be true. Yet, we seem to be so focused on what we put into something that we don't pay much attention to what the outcome is. Rich Warren (Warren 2002), also said, "Unexamined charity – a charity that fails to ask the hard questions about outcomes – only perpetuates poverty despite its best intentions. Responsible charity, on the other hand, engages not only the heart but the mind as well."

Lupton (Lupton 2015, 29-32) describes a two-day economic development summit he attended with urban ministry leaders from across the country. Most of the participants were non-profits: business-as-ministry enterprises to create jobs for unemployed residents in our depressed neighborhoods. The non-profits were far more ministry-minded than the handful of for-profits. However, none of the non-profits were turning a profit.

The for-profits rightfully felt that, while job training and job experience are certainly beneficial to employment and social services are necessary, none of that could happen without a wealth-creating community to support them. Non-profits were concerned about the slippery slope toward privilege and self-indulgence that wealth brings. They were focused on justice and equality. The business owners viewed profit as essential, good, and highly motivating. Both groups had to admit that wealth creation is the bedrock of economic vitality for any community, whether they liked it or not. They also agreed that communities needed both human services and wealth generators and that economic development is impossible without both.

Other Factors Affecting Accountability

Accountability doesn't exist in a vacuum. There are some very important considerations that need to be included as you seek to determine how you should be accountable. An expanded discussion follows in the respective Appendices:

1. Profit and Capital. Jesus' parable of the Talents focuses on what the managers had laid before them. We don't know a lot about

what instructions might have been given to these men, but we certainly know the outcome. Whatever capital we possess (see Appendix B), we should expect to use it faithfully in order to produce profit (or fruit or whatever).

2. Value. It is important to determine what value should be placed on whatever activity you engage in (see Appendix C). This is not necessarily the value you would place on it if you are doing something solely for yourself. It is the value that the person to whom you are accountable has placed on it. Value becomes part of the standard set for the conduct of the activity.

3. Government. In addition to the standards that have been set by Jesus, we are obliged to stay legal in our conduct as well. A discussion in Appendix D addresses how this affects operating in a business setting. Some people find it easy to "ease by" the regulations that have been imposed on many operations, and we cannot ignore them just because we are working for a "higher power."

We will be held to account for living up to what God has designed us to be. So, our responsibility is to find out what that calling is and to stay in constant prayer for God to lead you in ways that will enable you to do your best. That is what we are accountable for.

Chapter questions:

- The *steward* in Luke 16 was *held to account*. Have you faced such a situation?

- How do you view the responsibility of non-profits to be *accountable*?

- Why do you think that *accountability* doesn't show up on so many radar screens?

CHAPTER 4

THE BOTTOM LINE

Normally, what is considered to be the "crux (heart) of the matter" is referred to as "the bottom line." The Merriam Webster definition states: the bottom line is the **most important part of something**, the most important thing to consider, the final result or outcome, a company's profits or losses. In the end, it is what is created by the activity – good or bad.

Sometimes, we don't really care what the outcome turns out to be, but I would submit that it is not the norm. Let's say you are sitting on a recliner chair watching a movie on TV. It could very likely be that you don't care about the movie and you just don't have anything else to do. So, do you not have an outcome? You might not have an expected one, but you most probably will have some sort of outcome. Whether or not you like, dislike, or don't even care what the outcome is, there will be one or more. You may go to sleep, so the outcome is that you might get some rest. Unless you are a type A personality like I am, you could likely consider the outcome to be good. To me, rest is a necessity, not an outcome that I would seek just for the sake of it. I'm not saying that is good; I'm simply saying that there is an outcome, and the determination of the desirability of it is up to your intent or at least your opinion of it. I just don't like to have the burden of feeling that I wasted time. On the other hand, you and sometimes I find it entertaining or enlightening to watch a TV program. My outcome, and perhaps yours, could be to have something to consider or to discuss with others. If it is a sporting event, unless you have a wager on the outcome of it, you might just enjoy seeing your favorite team win or get some pleasure out of "bragging" about "our team" winning. In any of these cases, we desire a positive outcome.

If, by some unfortunate occurrence, we are interrupted, the outcome might become undesirable, negative, or unfruitful at the least. We might not care because it just gave us a chance to take a break from whatever we were doing. That, I would argue, possibly makes it positive. If it made you agitated because you didn't get to see the end of the program you were watching, your attitude could spill over into other activities. That happens to me all the time, just like it does when my favorite teams lose. That's when you need a cat to kick or whatever gives you release from your frustration.

Let's put the above scenario in a bit of a different light. My wife is not able to move around without someone else's help. If I sit down to watch TV when she is there (and awake), I am intending to have and desirous of having an outcome of sharing time with her. It is my choice to have that outcome, and I am investing time that I might be able to use more productively in a different activity to achieve it. I have also learned that I can accomplish the same thing by taking a break just to sit there for a while or work on my computer while watching TV (not always a good idea if you are watching a sporting event that you care about).

Counting the Cost

Jesus poses the question in Luke 14:28-30 regarding counting the cost of a project before you engage in it. He asks if a person would start out to build a tower without first considering the cost. He is pointing out what the negative outcome would be if the builder doesn't have enough money to complete it – his friends would laugh at him/her. For me, deriding "friends" would be the least of my concerns if I couldn't complete the project. My time and money are much too valuable to me to waste them on a foolhardy project. In verses 31-32, Jesus poses a similar but far more challenging matter to consider: a king sending out his warriors without regard to how many opposing warriors they would encounter. "Discretion is the better part of valor," as the saying goes. Perhaps Gen. Custer didn't attend that lesson at West Point!

WHERE I AM GOING WITH THIS IS TO ASK: DO YOU CONSIDER THE COST WHEN YOU ENGAGE IN A PROJECT? IF SO, DOESN'T THE BOTTOM LINE MATTER? THERE IS ALWAYS AN OUTCOME – A BOTTOM LINE.

The cost will be the main determining factor when looking at whether the outcome is worth undertaking. Will you have accomplished anything more than wasting time and spending money wrong-headedly?

You might think that this is rather elementary in considering important matters, but I have a few examples that might help drive my point home.

- An Indian school in Oklahoma asked churches to collect soup can labels to send in to help purchase a van they needed. I estimated that it would take hundreds of thousands of labels to reach the number required to qualify for the van. The effort alone makes it a very daunting task.

- Churches and other organizations were allowed to work in the bleachers' concession booths to get 15% of the sales for the days worked. All of us who worked there said we would just pay the amount we earned just to avoid doing it again.

- For two years I went on a mission trip to West Virginia (mentioned earlier). I was there working for a week each time, and it cost me about $600 (out-of-pocket costs) per trip. None of this went for materials, although the church did pay some out of the mission's budget. At 40 hours per week (I only worked about 20), that would have translated into $15 per hour worked. How much more benefit would that have been to an unemployed resident of the community? Now, I will freely admit that, on both occasions, I did have two of my grandsons with me. That was surely worth the cost, except that I could have worked on something closer to home and made more of a difference. The outcome wasn't worth it either in that

THE DIGNITY OF PROFIT
CREATING COMMUNITY THROUGH ENTREPRENEURSHIP

it just perpetuated a sense of dependency among the residents that it was supposed to help.

Accountability for the Bottom Line

The supreme irony of situation number 3 is that it has now been going on for over 20 years! Oh, it's not that it hasn't had some moments, but, on balance, I just don't see that the "bottom line" makes sense. Recently, I was at a leadership training ministry (LTM) event that preceded the start of a weekend experience. The pastor giving the message at the service that opened the training used the Luke 15 passage about the "Lost Sheep." (vv. 3-7) We had been lamenting the fact that the registrants for the weekend were quite low. His message was to let us know that, regardless of the number, we should make sure that the "one lost sheep" was rescued. I certainly got that, and I don't want to argue with Jesus. However, I don't think that I need to. The point, as I get it, is the *shepherd* left the sheep in the fold to go find the lost one. It would seem to me that there are better ways to reach that lost one than to throw an overwhelming number of witnesses at them. It's about the relationships that are built by such events, and there are those. Only I just see better ways to reach the lost.

What in the world does this have to do with the bottom line? To my way of thinking, the bottom line is creating disciples, and this has everything to do with that. Disciples answer the call from God to do whatever He has prepared them to do and to live up to that calling. The LTM should be very good at that, and in many cases (such as mine) it has worked.

I've been involved with the LTM for 18 years, and I have seen a lot of worthwhile results from their events. The community (as it is known) is very supportive of the program and the people who support it. I also know that there are places/examples where the program is still getting numbers that the program was designed to serve. Creating disciples has been referred to by many as multiplication. The aim of the program is to create what is known as *reunion groups*. The program is not doing enough the creation of reunion groups to create disciples. My point is that the bottom line is not appropriate for the activity that is being undertaken.

Is It Fair to Judge?

By now, you may be asking yourself: who is this idiot making such judgments? OK, fair enough. I have a right to my opinion, as do you. Frankly, I am writing this book to stimulate thinking about how the bottom line might more appropriately be considered. As we move into the next chapter, I would like to set the stage by stimulating your thinking in the direction of the bottom line that you are seeking. So much of what passes for bottom-line thinking is, in actuality, nothing more than an affinity for the activity itself.

Robert Lupton was cited in Chapter 2, where he states that between $2 billion and $5 billion is spent each year on mission-oriented trips to various places all over the globe. The activity is an industry in itself. The results are questionable. It would come as no secret that I believe the reason to be that most people are so eager to "do good" that they fall for groups that provide the opportunity to feed their passion. I guess I was jaundiced by what I saw when my kids went. I just couldn't see that the appropriate outcome was being considered. It is likely that the *desired* outcome is being achieved, or the ministry would not continue. That would be the outcome of getting people to go on the trips. This is not to say that the groups just want to take people's money. I'm willing to accept that they really think they are doing good themselves by helping others do good.

So now we swerved into determining people's motives, haven't we? Perhaps, but that is not my objective. Again, I am simply trying to change the narrative to focus on the *why* of decision-making. What I have observed is that we focus mainly on the *what* and the *how*. The why is generally just assumed: we are doing good by helping others to do good. Many of these activities/trips are cataloged, and would-be participants can peruse the catalogs to decide where they want to go. Arrangements are made much like planning a vacation. They are fairly well orchestrated, so savings on travel and lodging are achieved. Hopefully, there are meaningful activities available for the participants and there aren't more participants than can be effectively utilized.

I can tell you that, in many cases, there are challenging logistical issues that arise. It must be hard to make these activities work out to be as meaningful as would be desired. I mentioned earlier being on a couple of Habitat for Humanity experiences that were a bust, in part, because there were so many people as to make the project very inefficient. Certainly, Habitat is a very successful, worthwhile organization, and I support it enthusiastically. These were my experiences, and I have seen them happen on mission trips. It is primarily a consequence of using volunteer labor with varying skill levels. But the price is right, isn't it?

A big difference with Habitat is that it has clear objectives. While a lot of material and labor is donated, homeowners are required to put in "sweat equity." They do pay for the houses so that the funds are available to build more houses. Someone has oversight on the projects and areas are targeted rather than doing it on a hit-or-miss basis.

Food pantries are interesting situations. While the objective is to get food to the needy in an organized fashion, most of the pantries don't focus on trying to eliminate much of the need for the pantries by helping the "customers" change the situation that caused them to need free food in the first place. There are plenty of folks that, for whatever legitimate reason, need to be supplemented by the largess of these pantries. The problem is, for many of the pantries' patrons, getting to the point of being able to do for themselves is not a goal. By that, I mean pantries do not focus enough on truly assisting the needy that may not be able to do for themselves. Lupton has spent over 40 years in Atlanta, creating a new way of conducting food pantries. I invite you to visit his website, or better yet to get a copy of *Toxic Charity*. Others have begun to follow his example, and the way of operating food pantries has been changed for the good in several instances. Hopefully, many others will begin to see how they can enjoy the same kind of success. It's not easy to change minds and hearts, but I believe "...with God, all things are possible." (Matt.10:27)

In *Charity Detox* (Lupton 2015, 164-168), Lupton explains how to make a real difference by going to the next step of encouraging entrepreneurs to move into high-poverty areas to help revitalize the economic situation. Now, that's focusing on outcomes!

Only God knows people's hearts, and I refuse to engage in trying. However, it is appropriate to judge their actions – the law certainly does. As an entrepreneur and long-time business person, I have long been frustrated by those who engage in business-type transactions without proper training and intentions. It seems like I remember John Milton said that the road to hell is paved with good intentions – or something like that. Albert Camus is quoted as saying: "The evil that is in the world almost always comes of ignorance, and good intentions may do as much harm as malevolence if they lack understanding." I don't know if God grades on a scale that favors doing the right thing for the right reasons, but Lupton uses essentially the Hippocratic Oath when he includes "do no harm" in his "Oath for Compassionate Service." (Lupton 2011, 128). Perhaps I am just being naïve when I believe that people really want their efforts to have the most impact. Even so, I want to do what I can to help people change how they think and do compassionate service so that they can be reasonably certain that they are doing good in reality. Many people who have had experiences similar to mine have become disenchanted over the lack of impact their efforts have had. That gives me encouragement that I am onto something.

Albert Einstein said that doing the same thing over and over again and expecting different results is insanity. I would like to add that doing the same thing over and over again and not caring about the results is foolish – maybe even immoral! As I stated earlier, every endeavor has an outcome. This is what is generally known as the "bottom line." Whether or not it is profit (or one of the other synonyms) is up to a number of factors. If it is profit, it is a positive step toward the continuation – and hopefully expansion - of the enterprise.

Please don't misunderstand me. I have attempted to spell out the ways a positive bottom line can be attained. It may be the only outcome possible is *relationships*. To say this is not acceptable would be inaccurate. A caution should be offered is that they have to be the appropriate relationships. Specifically, if we are only reinforcing bad behavior or creating a relationship for our own benefit, we will not be considered to have had a positive outcome.

Chapter questions:

- Do you agree that every endeavor/project has a *bottom line* – gain or loss?

- Has your past experience has been with non-profits that only care if there is still money to spend? If so, can you see the importance of planning in order to show a gain at the end?

- Do you see how defining *success* can be critical to planning?

This marks the conclusion of Part I. It is intended to be the background necessary for engaging others about finding solutions to economic and spiritual growth in areas that have become disadvantaged for whatever reason.

Part II will take us to the heart of the problem, and we will determine what is likely to confront those who take it upon themselves to try to *make a difference.*

The Dignity of Profit

Part II:
What Is Going On?

CHAPTER 5

L.A.L.A. LAND

The Special Apple Tree

The apple tree is a fruit tree, but this story is about a very "special" fruit tree. The story is about a country long, long ago where the only fruit tree was the apple tree. In fact, it was the only one on the entire island where the country was located. The inhabitants existed on garden crops and livestock. The apples that came from the tree were kind of a special "treat." No one could remember how long the tree had been there – it had just always existed.

The best anyone could remember was that the island had been discovered so long ago that none of the original founders of the country were alive. No one really knew where they came from; they had been shipwrecked with no remains of the vessels. They had passed on some stories, but other than the livestock, the residents that remained only did what they knew to do.

The founders had brought the livestock with them, and the indigenous garden crops were there when they came. Those who were the farmers and livestock herders learned how to do the work of producing the crops and processing the meat that they ate and traded with each other.

The apple tree was the only tree on the island; they made their houses using stone, mud, and thatch. The weather was rather mild, and there was no need to be concerned about the cold or excessive heat. There was enough rain to water the crops and provide drinking water for the livestock and the residents.

The tree provided a treat for the residents and livestock. The apples were very sweet, and they were desired by the residents as the only "delicacy" available. There wasn't any need to do anything to tend the tree as it was mature and had reached the point where the annual crop was suitable for their needs. Life was good.

However, they began to take the tree for granted. They would pick a suitable amount for their needs, and the apples that fell to the ground were eaten by the livestock. They had learned how to take care of themselves, and the apples were just that something "special." No one tended the tree or cared to check to see if it needed any care. They just ate the apples or cooked them into some dish and then gave the peels and seeds to the hogs to eat.

Occasionally, people from the adjacent countries would come and pick some of the apples. At first, the neighbors were allowed to pick what they wanted. After all, the residents had more than they needed anyway. When the quantity of apples began to decline, however, the residents told the neighbors that they couldn't have apples any longer.

The neighbors still wanted the apples, so they offered to trade the residents something for apples. So, the residents decided that they could ration the apples that they ate in order to be able to accommodate the neighbors. No one knew exactly how to make a fair exchange, so they negotiated an amount of each that they could agree on and moved ahead with the process.

As fate would have it, the size of the harvest continued to decline. Therefore, the residents decided that they needed to have more in return for the apples. As the amount of the harvest declined further, so did the amount of the exchange required from the neighbors. The neighbors agreed for a time, but it was beginning to become a major irritant for them. The residents were enjoying the amount of return they were getting and didn't pay any attention to just how far the harvest was declining. Fortunately for the neighbors, fate stepped up again in the form of an innovator.

You see, the neighbors didn't have hogs, so they just threw the peels and seeds out in the garbage. The seeds began to sprout, and small apple trees began to grow. Having never had the experience, the innovator didn't know what to do with this find at first. He couldn't figure out if the small trees were a blessing or just an annoyance to get rid of.

As the innovator was considering the value of his find or the lack thereof, an entrepreneur came by. OK, he wasn't an entrepreneur yet because the entire island was just settling for things the way they were. So, this is like Sir Isaac Newton discovering gravity by being hit on the head by, of all things, an apple. The entrepreneur asked the innovator what the funny-looking growth was, and the innovator said he was just trying to figure it out himself. The entrepreneur pulled one out of the ground, and the innovator noticed that the growth was attached to an apple seed (he didn't really know what a seed was, but he had discovered that what was refused from the apples was the genesis of an apple tree).

The entrepreneur began to speculate as to whether the small growth would turn into an apple-bearing tree like the one that the residents had. He filed away the experience in the back of his mind and decided to wait to see what would happen. After the first year, some blooms appeared on the tree, along with some leaves. Still not able to determine if this had any prospects for him, the entrepreneur continued to wait. In the second year, he noticed that very small apples grew out of the blooms. They never got to the size that he had seen from the residents' tree, but waiting might be worth it to find out if this tree could really produce edible fruit. Sure enough, after a couple of more years, the tree grew substantially larger, and the fruit got larger as well.

This was their first "Ah, ha!" moment, and the wheels began to turn for them. The innovator was excited because he had made such a discovery, and the entrepreneur was planning how to profit from the discovery. As word spread around the village where this discovery was made, people began to picture the future (thanks to the entrepreneur) with their own apple trees and their own apples that they didn't have to pay a high price for.

This excitement did not derail the entrepreneur, however, because it takes a while for trees to get to the point where they actually produce apples, much less produce good apples. Most of the people were not interested in doing the work necessary to get trees to the point that the harvest was suitable. So, the entrepreneur and the innovator got together to start a nursery for apple trees.

Meanwhile, the other residents' harvest continued to decline, but they got wind of the efforts going on with the neighbors' plans. Instead of doing anything about the condition of the tree or learning from what the neighbors were doing, they continued to ration the crop so that they would have what they needed. The neighbors put up with it because their crop wasn't ready yet, and they found themselves desiring the apples more and more.

Then it happened: the residents' tree died. Near the end, they sold all of the harvests because they were losing interest in the apples due to the declining yield and the lack of interest from the neighbors in paying higher prices.

What was going on here?

1. God was not in this story. The people just struggled along on their own.

2. There was an absence of curiosity as to how to sustain the apple harvest.

3. Initially, the residents saw an opportunity by trading the apples with the neighbors.

4. Rationing seemed like a good answer to the dwindling harvest.

5. The entrepreneur saw an opportunity to revive the production and sale of the apples.

6. Over time, the residents' tastes changed because of the low yield.

7. At this point in the story, the neighbors were willing to let the innovator and the entrepreneur do the work and profit from their efforts/investment.

8. The purpose of apple trees is not to produce apples; it is to produce more apple trees.

9. Complacency is never a good plan – it actually isn't a plan.

10. A lack of curiosity will lead to future problems.

11. You should always pay attention to things that are going on around you. As Yogi Berra put it: "It is amazing what you can see just by looking."

12. Both innovators and entrepreneurs are necessary. Just because you discover something new doesn't mean that it is ready to be put into the stream of commerce.

13. The value of anything is what a willing seller will sell to a willing buyer for – or trade for.

14. Perseverance is an important component in reaching a successful outcome.

As I was writing this, there was a movie by this name that was contending for a Best Picture Oscar, along with many others. Along with the name of the city (Los Angeles), the title describes a place where we often feel that we are, and it is generally thought that this is a place where people just "don't get it." I'm not sure where this came from, but I made an acrostic that fits the concept:

(L)ethargic

(A)pathetic

(L) ackadaisical

(A)nti-capitalisitic

Not all of these are present in every situation, but it can be enough for only one to be a part of the mix. We will look at each of these and see what the impact can be of having one or more of them as an ingredient of the mindset of the residents.

So, we are going to take a trip to L.A.L.A. LAND. There we will investigate in order to determine what is going on there and what we can do about it (or them). As a consultant, it was my job to implement the plan that the analyst had determined to be the solution to the client's problem. We need to analyze the situation in the Land to properly plan the remedy. The remedy will lead to leadership training, planning the development of a community, and the creation and support of entrepreneurial ventures. It is important to have support from the residents to the extent that at least a desire exists to explore the possibility of joining together to attack the problem.

The problem with "buy-in" is that most of us don't recognize that we have a problem. Television "sit-coms" are normally scripted around dysfunctional families. They may not be traditional families (M.A.S.H. comes to mind, as well as *That 70's Show* and others), but they have some sense of people living together in the same facility. They share things in common, and they display all the difficulties of being related to each other. However, most people who venture to watch those things are usually unaware of the character that reflects them. The ones that can identify closely with the particular show's premise seem to find plenty to be amused about. My guess is they see themselves as the most favorable character of the lot. *Home Improvement* is one that I like (it's still in syndication). However, my daughter has said that I remind her of the Tim Allen character because I have so many "accidents." Personally, I couldn't see it.

THE POINT IS, WHEN YOU COME TO TELL PEOPLE THAT THEY HAVE A PROBLEM, MUCH OF THE TIME, THEY WILL TELL YOU THAT THEY DON'T.

A story in John 5:3-9 tells where Jesus encountered a man that had been sick for 38 years and was waiting by the pool for someone to help him get in it. One would think that over a period of time that he had been there, someone would have been willing to help the man. It is interesting that Jesus asked the man: "Do you want to get well?" That's an interesting question; shouldn't it be obvious? Well, Jesus certainly knew something (of course He did). Perhaps the man was afraid of taking a chance. The reason he was there in the first place was the belief that when the water became agitated, a person who was in the water could be healed. It is amazing what we can talk ourselves into – or out of. Holding onto hope is something that we do if we find ourselves in difficult situations. We tend to hold onto something that gives us hope, even when we don't have a good reason to.

There will be a lot more about this later, but you should be aware people don't recognize what is going on around them just like fish don't understand the concept of water. You may have gained all the knowledge and experience, but there has to be an awareness of the problem before people will accept your advice and help.

The Journey Begins

Given my comments above, I hope you will appreciate the importance of having an "invitation." By that, I mean that you should avoid descending on an unsuspecting populace. As much as you may want to take on a perceived problem, you should resist the temptation. I'm reminded of the story of the Boy Scouts that were sent out to see how they might do their daily "good turn." When the day was over, and the groups had returned, the time had come to report on their experiences. One of the groups was reporting their successes, and one of them was a bit suspicious. The first scout announced that he had helped an old lady across the street. One by one, the rest of the group got up and reported the same thing. Becoming a bit skeptical about this, the leader asked the group where they found so many old ladies. The response was that it was actually the same one. The leader then asked why it took all of them to help one old lady across the street. The answer was that the lady didn't want to go!

This is a silly story, but it does illustrate the problem that is created when you try to force your desires on someone else. The irony is most of the time, it is the symptoms that prompt people to seek help. If they knew how to deal with the problem, they would do it themselves. Those who try are not usually that successful in correcting the situation.

Although I spoke of L.A.L.A. Land in the beginning, that is normally not the source of the problem. I chose an area to begin the process of determining how to be of service to my fellow entrepreneurs. This area was rather typical of many rural areas, and the residents that I spoke with all indicated that the problem was the lack of jobs. Now, it's not that there were jobs, but the lack of them was symptomatic of a different problem. What it didn't take long for me to learn was that people didn't want jobs. So, businesses that might be interested in locating in the area couldn't find willing and able workers to employ. Some felt that the lack of jobs was primarily due to the breach of a large dam that provided electrical power for the major utility. Several businesses closed, and they were not reopened or sold to anyone. It turns out that we have one problem feeding the other.

The capital base of the area I mentioned had declined as houses were not kept up and couldn't be sold anyway. This area is like many that have seen a dramatic event disrupt what had seemed to be healthy before it. This is sometimes referred to as the "tipping point." That is when the proverbial straw breaks the camel's back. It is not uncommon for the folks involved in such a scenario to be blissfully ignorant of the impending storm. You may walk a tightrope when you try to help them come to understand the gravity of the situation.

This is the story of much of rural America today. Over time, the local economy has devolved mightily from what it once was. My hometown has experienced that phenomenon. Little by little, the town lost businesses, and the population plummeted. Of course, growing up, I never intended to go back home after I finished college. Several of my contemporaries did, however. Many of them still live in the area, but their children didn't go to the school that we all did. Not long after I went to college, desegregation caused parents to pull their children out of the public schools. The building where I attended elementary school was turned over to a private school. That didn't last long, and then there was none. The entire county schools were integrated, and new buildings were built. Today, the county unemployment rate is about 28%.

The situation in the area where I chose to locate my ministry is not nearly to that point, but the future doesn't look that great either. The settlement from the utility company following the dam breach brought a lot of money that has been spent on rehabilitation, but a sizeable amount is still available. Attempts have been made to determine the most beneficial use of the remaining funds. This included some consulting engagements, meetings with local opinion shapers, and funding individual projects. The major challenge that remains is to change the attitude that a majority of the residents have that the things in the county are "OK."

In many of these areas, the school district is the largest employer in town. This has been the case for many years, and it is not getting better for most places. The death spiral looks a little like this in many areas:

1. Unless there has been a major event in the community, the school district may languish around a certain enrollment level until such an event comes along or attrition sets in.

2. Retirements follow graduations which means that there are those who move away after their child graduates, or they become no longer interested in the district and its activities.

3. Even an excellent school district will now find it difficult to replace the people who are retiring or leaving.

4. Aging citizens move out of independent living situations, leaving houses that need lots of work and cannot be rehabbed at a reasonable cost.

5. Business owners age as well and cannot sell a business that hasn't been kept up in recent times. This affects not only the owners themselves, but the loss of business activities and tax revenues further degrades the local economy – including the schools.

6. In some areas, the government takes land for its use thereby taking it off the tax rolls. Although funds are usually provided to counties to make up for some of this loss, overall tax collections in the state can affect the amounts they receive.

7. Not only are schools unable to attract employees (mainly teachers), but the economy doesn't attract families with children of school age.

8. In order to acquire the funds necessary to keep schools open, the districts institute programs that may not help local residents. Specifically, in many areas, the programs are training students for jobs that don't exist in the local economy.

The result is unless something is done to change this spiral, towns will dry up as education is only provided in larger areas that do nothing to support the community where they live.

Preparation is the key, and there are various components of the background that should be considered before appearing on site. The first stop is at the city of "attitudes" that are behind the words of L.A.L.A. Land.

ATTITUDES

This is really a very large city that is interspersed with characteristics that themselves, describe the city. The reason that I refer to this as "a very large city" is that many areas are suffering from the collective attitudes that are included. Any one of them is enough to derail efforts to assist the residents to make their lives better. Changing these attitudes is quite difficult due to the legacy that has been passed down from generation to generation.

Motivational speaker and author Jim Rohn wrote in a newsletter that "having the right attitude is one of the basics that success requires. The combination of a sound personal philosophy and a positive attitude about ourselves and the world around us gives us an inner strength and a firm resolve that influences all the other areas of our existence." I have also heard it said that your attitude is really the only thing that you have control over. Rohn mentions a lot about the negative effects that attitude can have on your life as well.

Christian Schwarz, creator of the Natural Church Development (NCD) program, uses a survey to assess churches on eight "Quality Characteristics." Based on the score that churches give themselves on these, he offers tests and books to assist churches to improve the respective area. While I was trained on the program and worked with a church that was using the program, I was only later given books by Schwarz for use in developing community and effective leadership. Looking at these particular areas was eye-opening for me, as I had not done so when working with the church.

Both of these books (as well as some others designed to address other characteristics) included a test to help focus on particular attitudes that can either enhance the possibility of improving deficiencies or making them worse. Schwarz supports the notion that building community is very important to being able to accomplish anything that positively impacts the organization. As he concludes the book on community, he strongly recommends the leadership test and prescriptions as well. I found both books and prescriptions to be quite sound and to have application in any organizational setting. The reason for this is that they require a gifts assessment to determine how the person can be most effective in their endeavors.

My point in this is that I have found that prescriptions are important in directing the steps to be taken to implement the solution. Schwarz has given a God-based means of approaching the pathway to success. After we prepare you for your visit to the city of *Attitudes*, we will have a visit to *History*. There, we will point out how things got the way they are.

Lethargic

Merriam-Webster's definition of the word lethargy includes the quality or state of being lazy, sluggish, or indifferent. Some synonyms are languor and stupor. These suggest that there is inertia or listlessness from either internal or external sources. Depression is one of the most common illnesses that contributes to the condition. The external forces can be just as pervasive. There are a whole host of antonyms that illustrate how much of a problem this can be: eagerness, enthusiasm, keenness, spiritedness, ambition, enterprise, vim, vigor, and vitality. These are words that can be used to describe passion. So, it is logical to believe that lethargy is a lack of passion. Dr. Phil McGraw says that passion is what gets you up in the morning.

People, by nature, tend to get comfortable with things they know. This is true even if the situation they find themselves in is less than optimum. Part of it is probably due to a fear of the unknown, and change is not high on the list of desirability. Regardless of the reason, making progress depends on a willingness to take on something new or different.

Philip Crosby provided his Theory of Human Behavior: People subconsciously retard their own intellectual growth. "They rely on clichés and habits. Once they reach the age of their own personal comfort with the world, they stop learning, and their mind runs idle for the rest of their days. They may progress organizationally, they may be ambitious and eager, and they may even work night and day. But they learn no more." Admittedly, this is a rather bleak assessment; however, the point is a critical one. This seems to be more prevalent in bureaucratic scenarios. The military is a prime example of the extent to which this can go. There are regulations for virtually everything, and those in charge are responsible for ensuring complete adherence to these. The need to very strictly "follow the rules" is fairly obvious in such situations. The unfortunate thing is that people get so fixed on the rules and regulations that they don't do a very good job of thinking. Most governmental agencies lean heavily on them, and it slows the operation immensely.

The paradox is that, as a military pilot, you are, on the one hand, absolutely required to know what to do when operating an aircraft, while on the other hand, there is a lot that has to be done in case of emergencies. Basically, in the first case, you must do things without thinking, and in the second case, you must be able to react instinctively. While there is some flexibility in the process, for the most part, everything is expected to follow guidelines. The problem comes when people higher up the "totem pole" get so fixated on rules and regulations that operations become stagnated.

There are lots of experiences that I could relate to, and readers probably have many as well. The effect this has on communities trying to secure funding for projects from governmental agencies or even private foundations is to squash initiative. The benefit I mentioned earlier from the breach of a dam has been almost imperceptible due to the process being slow in distributing the funds and the lack of interest in rebuilding by most of the businesses that had been affected. Couple that with the endemic poverty and dependency on public assistance, and you will find a population that generally has little or no interest in changing things.

Earlier, I mentioned John 5, where we were introduced to a situation that Jesus faced at the pool in Bethesda. We don't really know exactly how this affected the man going forward. Jesus didn't preach the man a sermon, and we are not told that he went about sharing the news with others. Maybe this lesson is to show people how we are to respond to such situations.

What this means is that if you are trying to make a difference in either your own life or the lives of others, you will certainly encounter the pitfall of lethargy. An additional path needs to be considered if this is true for your personal life. It is not my intent to deal with that. If you are in a condition of being lethargic, you quite probably wouldn't have begun to read this book, and I'm pretty sure that you wouldn't have gotten this far if you did. The experience you most likely will have is finding people in a particular area or grouping that are "plateaued out."

It's somewhat like the "Peter Principle" that was set forth by Dr. Laurence Peter in an article in Esquire magazine in 1967. His contention was that in a person's career, people tend to get promoted until they reach their "level of incompetence." He put it more simply by saying cream rises to the top until it sours. The business world found the idea/article so compelling that they co-opted the idea. It became so popular that Dr. Peter wrote a book entitled *The Peter Principle: Why Things Always Seem to Go Wrong*. While most used this to blame management for not doing their homework, some saw this as more of a condition affecting the behavior of the employee (the person) themselves. They pointed out that many employees manipulate the reward system to boost themselves into a position for a promotion. Having achieved it, they tend to level off (or plateau). Elsewhere, I have made my thoughts plain about the issues that are a part of bureaucracies. The Peter Principle is alive and thriving in most of them.

Going back to the beginning of this section, both scenarios are part of the lethargy that I am writing about. If the passion is missing in action or has died somewhere along the way, the effect is the same. This is a major hurdle to overcome if you are trying to help make a difference in the lives of the community. Passion can be infectious or it can be off-putting. It can be very helpful to have someone that you can share your passion with. It's also pretty important to have a person who is a native or long-time resident to be your "partner" in these endeavors. This can be challenging sometimes, but what I have found is that somehow breaking through the barrier is what is critical to being successful. It's been said that getting other people to do what you want them to do is one of the hardest things you can do in life. Couple this with the lethargy thing, and you can be trying to climb a steep hill.

Apathetic

It has been said that the opposite of *love* is not *hate*; it is *greed*. The encounter Jesus had with the rich ruler in Mark 10:17-31 shows that having *everything* tends to make one greedy, but, to me, greed at least leads to *apathy*. However, the rich themselves are not the only ones that can be apathetic about those in need. James 2:2-7 tells of how partiality gets shown preferential treatment and the poor get shoved aside. On the other hand, in verse 5, James specifically says that God has chosen the poor to be rich in faith and heirs of the Kingdom. Lest I be unkind to those who are very philanthropic, many wealthy people give much of their wealth and even of themselves.

In His Steps by Charles Sheldon was the beginning of WWJD – what would Jesus do? It is a fictitious account of a church in an inner-city location that had to be awakened to the poverty and injustice around them. Most of the members really weren't "bad" people; they just weren't paying attention to the world around them. I think God sends us opportunities to increase our awareness of the needs that may be just outside our doors – figuratively speaking, perhaps. The challenge we have is paying attention and then acting appropriately. We'll deal with that in another section, but overcoming our inertia is where we are called to act.

The first line of Rick Warren's *Purpose Driven Life* is: "It's not about you." Most of the book speaks of how we need to put ourselves in a lesser position, a servant as Jesus put it. Apathy doesn't have a direct connection to selfishness, but my guess is that being self-absorbed makes us less likely t be concerned about others.

Lackadaisical

OK, this may be close to *lethargic* and there weren't any other "L" words that would fit. There is a difference – albeit a fine one. In a narrow definition, *lackadaisical* means "Lacking enthusiasm and determination; carelessly lazy." Whereas *lethargy* suggests that a person is just practically devoid of energy, I see *lackadaisical* as being at a different level with energy but without any drive or direction. This seems to be just sort of floating along, letting life take you where it will go. It may not be a problem to be a trash collector and let a little bit of trash fall out when emptying the can. On the other hand, if you are working with precision tolerances, being lackadaisical can lead to disastrous results.

It's not just being careless and lacking determination; the enthusiasm gap can cause a person to miss a lot of opportunities. It seems to me that lethargy can come from a lack of passion about much of anything. Being lackadaisical suggests that change is perhaps out of the realm of interest. Where this comes into play in community development projects is in whether you can expect folks to be interested in much of anything vs. doing something new and different that could lead to improvement.

What I have observed is a sort of plateauing effect where no interest in advancement exists. One way to describe such people is that they are "settlers." It's pretty easy to see how this fits: folks just seem to become satisfied with things the way they are. The man that Jesus encountered by the pool at Bethesda must have become somewhat satisfied. After all, he had been sitting by the pool for 38 years and hadn't been healed. That's an example of perseverance, but it gets worse. When Jesus asked the man if he wanted to be well, he gave the excuse that no one had carried him to the pool. The man obviously did want to be made well; Jesus healed him on the spot. If Jesus had carried him to the pool, the message would have been that the legend was true.

I once heard Kenneth Bailey on Christian radio speak of matters such as this. He was the author of a book, *Jesus Through Middle Eastern Eyes*, and said that it was actually a job that some people had to be beggars. According to him, Jews were obliged to give alms to the poor, and particularly blind people were accepting their handouts to help them fulfill that.

The problem comes when things don't stay the same. In the area I have described elsewhere, even with a sizeable award from the electric utility company, the "restoration" is extremely slow. Things weren't great to start with (at the time when the breach occurred), but within the past five years, several additional businesses have closed. The attitude is that, for the most part, the award should be spent on things that won't do much, if anything, to improve the economic climate. Attracting new businesses into the county has not been a productive endeavor due to the "settler" mentality that still exists. Many of the residents are hoping to get a factory to return that closed before the Vietnam War! The area has heavy tourist traffic, but very little retail business exists. Most of the existing businesses don't care about tourist trade anyway.

So maybe the difference here is that lackadaisical is probably better defined as "intellectual laziness." It seems that a lot of people just don't think very deeply about things. I may be guilty of doing just the opposite; I am so curious that I just can't stand to be uninformed about things that come across my radar screen. That's not to say that I am well-informed about a lot of things. I remember my mother relating to me the results of an IQ test I had when I was in one of the lower grades in school. There is probably some point that it becomes valid to determine such things. It was probably then that I was tested along with my classmates. Anyway, the result basically pointed out that I knew a little about a lot of things. When just about everything in the world is new to you, curiosity can overwhelm you. If I am indeed "guilty" of being a deep thinker, there must be an accumulation of information-gathering that contributed to it.

When I noticed eyes glazing over when I was speaking on some topic, I realized that I had gone beyond the limits of what people cared to hear about. Some people are just anal-retentive like I am and either want to be an authority on things or just don't like to be wrong. I just seem to have this uncontrollable desire to comment on matters that interest me. When I do, I want to be well-informed, so I watch the internet, looking up things that interest me. It has helped immensely in being able to form an opinion about a matter and then be able to back it up with facts. The problem is that an awful lot of people just accept things that make sense without doing any research. Wrong notions can be entrenched that way, and it is difficult to get through to them with a valid argument.

An example in the case of rural communities is the fact that they are very protective of the land that they own. Additionally, they generally don't want their neighbors to sell the land they own either. It may be that they are concerned that land will be taken out of farm production. It probably means that there would be a lot of new folks around, crowding them in the stores and common areas. What they don't realize is that, in many cases, the largest demographic- and the only one that is growing – is adults 65 years old and over. The impact of this is felt by every citizen whether they know it or not. It is the decline of the capital base, which is not supporting services and not attracting new residents out of concern for property values declining further.

Anti-Capitalistic

The Presidential election of 2016 was an interesting time in a myriad of ways – an understatement of the century. From time to time, there have been businesspeople who have served in political office, but the presidency has been one that has not drawn the right mix of people's desires and qualified candidates. There have been military leaders who have made it, but it was understandable in a time when there were struggles for power around the world that the U.S. had some interest in. With a country that is over $20 trillion in debt and coming off an eight-year tenure of a president where there was 2% GDP growth or less, people have recognized the need for someone to lead the country that knows how to make good business decisions. The unfortunate reality is that those who didn't support the ultimate decision on who would be president had a lot of trouble accepting the fact that there was tremendous discontent in the land.

The problem with characterizing a particular area as being *anti-capitalistic* is that it is a very pervasive attitude in the U.S. I hesitate to come down too hard on this condition because it is so common. The point is that we have slowly let an anti-capitalistic mentality creep up on us. Early in the 20th century, John Maynard Keynes came up with a theory that became almost "gospel" to many economists and politicians. It has led to a strong leaning toward a reliance on government for far too many things.

The major problem with the anti-capitalistic mentality is that, since it essentially started with the movement toward socialism, the real growth is now with the people who espouse socialistic views. Also, since entrepreneurship is not in great favor with socialists, small business growth is hampered by the expansion of socialist ideals. How is it that folks like Mark Zuckerberg, the Facebook founder and CEO, are pushing the idea of a minimum income for all citizens? They wouldn't have to do anything to get it, but they can work if they want to. Zuckerberg says that this would free entrepreneurs to be creative without being concerned with setbacks. One concept is that innovators can create robots to do all the work while they enjoy the benefits of their creations. I'm just not sure how this works. One viewpoint I have heard was that "sloth had become sexy." I guess we don't have to worry about defending our way of life because it won't be defensible if we don't have anything but robots to defend us – especially if they can be hacked into by our enemies.

This isn't a new concept, it turns out. A project going on in Finland involves more than 20,000 people that receive the minimum income. Supposedly, Finland can't fill the available jobs, so they believe this will encourage people to work for more if they don't have the high welfare payments they are currently receiving. Huh? I was shocked to hear that Thomas Paine wrote some of the same things in *The Rights of Man*. I wasn't shocked to hear that President Franklin Roosevelt advocated it in a speech he gave entitled *Freedom from Want*. I would argue that those who espouse such views must not really care much about other people.

Ludwig von Mises gave a very interesting (and I believe accurate) account of how socialism got its start. He goes back to the days of feudal times to describe the situation for the people who were artisans of the times. Basically, these people had no income except for being supported by royalty. The royals had pride in the quality of the work of these artisans. In those times, there was essentially no economic benefit to the kingdom from these artisans, and they were always "on the bubble" in terms of performing well enough to continue in the employ of the royalty. Nicolai Lenin seized on the fact that there were workers who were uneasy with the conditions of their working situation. This was coupled with the non-production workers who felt that they were due more for the contribution they made to the process. Entrepreneurialism was not encouraged and didn't really exist in such environments except in farming. It seems to me that governments (even those who "encourage" entrepreneurism) are more interested in having large corporations since they employ more people. Trade unions took the place of the sole proprietors in many industries. In this way, more control could be exerted by the sheer number of employees involved, and there was more at stake in retirement and unemployment funds.

Robert Lupton says that the world is awakening to the reality that healthy economic systems are fundamental to the elimination of poverty. Looking back to Chapter 2, you can hopefully see that we need a theological balance in our understanding of wealth. If some of the more resourced members of the wider church were to step forward, the church could see itself with a much broader role. Perhaps it could see itself as not just a purveyor of compassionate services but also a catalyst for fruitful economies. This could be the way to start to bring economic wholeness to struggling souls too long resigned to unending poverty.

While the effects of this attitude are mostly felt at a higher level than local communities, the way it manifests itself locally is in the individual's reliance on government "entitlements." So, the politicians create the programs to "benefit" those in need. On its face, these programs are necessary and truly help the recipients. Beneath the surface, however, much harm has been done through the dependency that results from such largess. How this trickles down from the initial benefit derived from the program has been addressed elsewhere.

The Enormous Impact of L.A.L.A. Land

Government

Many areas are second and third-generation recipients of government handouts. Nicholas Eberstadt in *Men without Work*, lays out how the way our economy has shifted its approach to unemployment helped to create the problem we have. Not only have the numbers been inaccurately reported to make government efforts to improve the situation appear more effective, but the chronic nature of unemployment has also permeated the attitude of increasing numbers of men of prime working age. Here are some of the effects of government's involvement:

1. Healthcare – In Bill Clinton's first term, his wife, Hillary, took on the task of coming up with what can best be described as "universal health care." It was a disaster, and it showed how

unattractive government involvement in such matters can be. However, in 2009, in Barack Obama's first term, the Democrats had majorities in the U.S. House of Representatives and in the U. S. Senate, and they passed the Affordable Care Act (aka: Obamacare). Republicans tried every way they could to get the law repealed, but Obama rejected all of their attempts. One of Donald Trump's campaign pledges was to repeal and replace the law. When he was elected, he enjoyed a majority in both houses of Congress, and he immediately undertook the challenge of making good on his pledge. Early attempts haven't worked, so it remains to be seen if it will happen. Columnist Charles Krauthammer assessed the situation quite well when he said that Obamacare had created a sense of entitlement among the American people when it comes to healthcare. The intent was to move the country to universal healthcare, and the Democrats are struggling with trying to make that work.

2. Education – on all sides of the matter (and there are plenty) many programs have been tried to improve the U.S. education system. Very few of them have made any real difference. The president of ABC in the 1980s summed it up pretty well when it comes to discussions about how to improve the system when he said: "After all is said and done, more will be said than done." My wife was a teacher, and I taught at the college level for a few years. Most of my good experience came from selling educational computer systems to schools. There was skepticism about "new things," of course, and there was a lot of ignorance about what such systems could actually do. For the most part, the technology is still underutilized.

3. What bothers me more, however, is that schools are driven by programs that provide money to conduct. Examples are especially true in the trade areas (masonry, welding, etc.). Almost all of the ones I know are not tied to specific industry needs – at least not in the location where they are offered. Consequently, students get trained for jobs that don't exist, only not where they live. It would be fine if these people went elsewhere to work, but many of them don't. The programs that I have seen work are company-specific so that they can

expect to work at that company if they meet the requirements to complete the training.

4. Support of business activities – The government decides, from time to time, that there are specific industries that need to be supported in order to benefit the population at large. Some of the ones that have been included over the years are energy (solar, wind power, waste), transportation (oil and gas, emissions, mileage), safety (Environmental Protection Agency projects, automobile safety, and a million other areas), food (health-related items and protection of crops). In most cases, getting the government involved means that more government workers get hired and costs for the items they are focusing on cost more.

5. Welfare and disability – What can I say about these? Add to these unemployment benefits and you have a major drain on tax revenues. Entitlements between 1960 and 2010 grew from 19% of all U. S. government spending to 43%. The rate of non-entitlement to entitlement spending fell from 4.2:1 to 1.3:1. Most of the categories of entitlements can be put into six overall baskets: income maintenance, Medicare, Medicaid, Social Security, unemployment insurance, and all others.

6. Small Business Administration – In the way of full disclosure, I had a loan from the SBA, and they were probably the most helpful of all the players in that comic opera. The "collections guy" gave me the best deal I could get in order to maintain the loan until I got the building sold and got a payout on the rebates that were being held by the cooperative I belonged to. He even testified at that trial, where I sued the bank and my former partner. However, the first person that handled my case was overwhelmed and really didn't care about my situation or any of the others he was handling at the time. He just wanted to pass my case on. The next two people I met with could only tell me how the deck was stacked against me. Actually, what that did for me was to give me the determination to make them wrong by working my way out of the situation I was in.

My attorney told me about a situation he was called into. The SBA wanted to make a direct loan to a person who was looking to purchase an auto parts business. It turns out that all my attorney was supposed to do was rubber stamp the inventory value so the loan could be made. What he found was minimum saleable merchandise and six obscure Dodge engines. My attorney refused to certify the value, but someone did it. I don't know whether the business made it or not, but that action diverted funds from the pool that could have helped legitimate businesses.

Another thing that gave me the motivation to avoid default was that I had essentially pledged everything but the family dog to collateralize the loan. A company I worked for once defaulted, and the SBA took everything.

There are several reasons that government involvement is causing problems with the general populace. The major one, to my way of thinking, is taking away the *dignity* of those who are receiving something from the government. At one point, I was laid off from one job and basically living off what I was making from a small business. Mind you, this business was intended to be a supplement to my regular income, but the layoff changed that. I learned that I could qualify for free or reduced lunches for my kids at school. My first shock was that I qualified. The next shock was that I never expected that to be the case for me. At that time in my life, I had been through the loss of a lawsuit that I had brought against my former partner and my former bank, the loss of an infant child, and near bankruptcy. When I told my son that I had lost my job, he was afraid that he might have to drop out of college. One might think that I wouldn't have any dignity left to be concerned about, but to me, that is one of the things that you don't want to lose. Just so you know, I didn't take the lunch "entitlement."

During the "Great Recession," unemployment benefits were extended to 99 weeks. I never knew how they came up with that. It was probably that the computers didn't have room for three digits in the "months" field. Anyway, I had a friend who was laid off, and his wife came to a prayer group I was in. She was concerned that he had been laid off for almost two years and didn't have much hope of getting a job. I spoke with him later and expressed my concern and offered to pray for him. He chuckled and said that he wasn't looking because he still had benefits left. By the way, he got a job almost immediately after the 99 weeks ran out.

Churches don't help with this situation. I have known of some organizations that meet in churches such as *Businesspersons Between Jobs.* Mostly, though, churches seem to either exacerbate the situation by handouts or simply provide sympathy. When I was involved in the situation, I mentioned that it involved near bankruptcy, my pastor asked me to be in charge of the *Pony Express* (a creative method for raising money for pledges to the church budget.) I told him that I was in the middle of rather desperate circumstances and didn't think I could take this one. He said that he didn't know how to help me – then he wouldn't take "no" for an answer on the fund-raising drive. That helped me to realize how much I could handle. Of course, that was because I was trusting God, and I knew that He would get me through.

Attitude Shift

"Attitude is a habit of thought – if you want to change your attitude, you must change the way you think." (Paul J. Meyer). In Scripture, we find in Phil. 2:5 "Your attitude should be the same as that of Christ Jesus." There are some fields of endeavor that demand a positive attitude. Athletes and salespeople certainly know that. If they don't, they won't be successful. However, they know that it has to be internalized. You can't just say positive things; you have to be able to live what you believe.

It has been accurately said that we act out of what we believe. People are willing to do amazing things based on a belief that they are acting out of truth. Think about it: people jump on zip lines if they believe that it is safe. Attitude connects to determination. If you feel that you are the best at something, you will likely be determined to prove it. Proverbs 23:7 tells us that as a man "thinks in his heart, so is he." We are what we are, not what we appear to be. It is because of the thoughts that dominate our minds.

Meyer also says that your overall pattern of thinking is generally positive or negative. This attitude affects several things in your life, and one of them is how you see opportunity. Negative thinking "buries" the ability to see opportunity. A positive attitude opens your mind to so many opportunities; the challenge is to decide which one to pursue.

Attitudes develop over time, and it takes time to change them. Of course, change is not going to occur unless you have made the decision to change. Once you have made that decision, the methodology of change is the same as how they were created in the first place:

- **Sow a thought, reap an action**
- **Sow an action, reap a habit**
- **Sow a habit, reap a character**
- **Sow character, reap a destiny**

The Significance of a Positive Attitude

Certainly, I have pointed out the challenge of dealing with prevailing attitudes in the areas that we are seeking to help. Over time, the people who remain in areas affected by stagnant growth or lack of growth have settled into a sense of complacency that reflects their negative attitudes. As the previous section on L.A.L.A. Land points out, these attitudes are the reason for no growth. All but one of these attitudes display a lack of interest in doing things any differently. The other one is actually anti-growth with respect to the general economy. Of course, in reality, anything that does not support growth has a negative effect on it. Nothing stays the same regardless of how people view it.

David Smick, author of *The Great Equalizer*, points out that a new attitude is necessary for people to be interested in innovating again. It may come on its own, which is not uncommon following a period of growing income inequality. It may come from people feeling they are being left behind. When the U.S. has found itself lagging behind other nations, citizens have stepped up to meet the challenge. It is not so much a desire to help the nation's economy; it reflects the desire to find a way to better their personal situation. As Smick describes, however, innovators have stepped up when they feel that they are on their own. That's actually not a bad thing as a top-down economy seldom spreads the wealth to the ones who need it most.

THE AVERAGE PERSON DOESN'T REALLY STAND A

CHANCE WHEN IT COMES TO INVESTING IN THE STOCK MARKET OR OTHER PLACES THAT ARE MANIPULATED BY INSTITUTIONAL INVESTORS. THE BEST PLACE FOR THEM TO CAST THEIR LOT IS WITH INVESTMENTS THAT ARE CLOSER TO HOME, SO TO SPEAK.

Bottom-up growth will have more effect on the well-being of the average person than waiting for things to get better by trickling down. The best way to make a local economy stronger is to build a sense of community – helping people understand that they are in it together (see Chapter 6). For the most part, attracting capital and revenue from outside of the community will help strengthen it as well. Building a strong capital base has many benefits.

When you look at much of rural America, you see many empty buildings where businesses have once been housed. In some cases, this is due to what is referred to as the "Wal-Mart effect." However, while Wal-Mart doesn't necessarily destroy local businesses, it does change it. There are certainly cases when a Wal-Mart closes or moves to another location, causing a negative effect. People get used to the donations that Wal-Mart makes and the tax revenues that it brings in. With very little going on in these communities, housing values drop as well. This begins to erode schools and services important for a community to be a desirable place to live and work. I wrote of this spiral early in the chapter.

When people have seen things only get worse, they tend to lose hope. Attitudes reflect this, but they can be changed. The presidential election of 2016 showed a push-back from people who were tired of seeing things deteriorate. It remains to be seen if the attitude of the people at the community level changes enough to strengthen the economic base of these areas.

An Attitude of Gratitude

It is not surprising that people would become disillusioned by events over the past 50 years or so. Factories have closed, and many have moved overseas. Jobs that were once secure no longer exist.

Mergers and acquisitions have ripped the economic heart out of many communities. Tastes change, and innovations come on the scene that render products and businesses obsolete. Efficiencies created by new methods have eliminated jobs. Education has not kept up with the needs of a 21st-century economy. Government reacts to these changes by providing welfare programs that create a disincentive to work.

So, what is there to be grateful for? The Apostle Paul's first letter to the Thessalonians says that we are to give thanks in everything (5:18). The fact is that we almost always have many things to be thankful for. However, Jesus said several times that we should rejoice in suffering and tribulation. These things produce character if we learn from them rather than wallow in our desire for pity. If we suffer for the Kingdom, we will have great rewards in Heaven. Scripture tells us that after we "have suffered a little while, the God of all grace, who has called (us) to His eternal glory in Christ, will Himself restore, confirm, strengthen, and establish you." I can attest to having found blessing in adversity and finding rewards in being faithful. Each time, there has been strength that I found in Christ that helped me to face difficulties in the future.

Positive people see opportunities in all situations and never have a "bad day." In many cases, this comes from knowing that God cares for us and wants the best for us. If difficulties come their way, they deal with them and don't let them get them down. I have even laughed at things that seem to just "come out of left field" and wonder how God is going to deal with them. It wasn't always the case with me, but since I have learned to trust God in such situations, I have seen how much better it was when I did.

A New Way to View Attitudes About Economics

Attitudes usually develop early in life. We are seeing the way communication in all forms is being pushed lower and lower on our youth. Home situations may not be positive. Divorce rates are higher than ever, and people seem to be more self-focused than ever. It seems that at this point, we have lost a generation of our youth and are in danger of losing another one. How can we turn this around?

Both Smick and Jim Chilton, author of *The Coming Jobs War*, contend that we have to address the problem of how to change the future economic picture by getting our youth involved early-on. Neither of them suggests that the church has the solution, but I have seen that it can, at least, be a strong partner in finding it. This involved including youth in housing rehab projects and helping them start craft-type businesses. Helping people who are in need and helping youth learn how to do for themselves are two very powerful ways that can change attitudes for the better.

Jim Chilton, the Chairman of the Gallup organization, has done surveys on all sorts of things for many years. His book cited above is a description of their 21st-century way of looking at economics. A very compelling case is made for abandoning the way that predictions have been made about economics in the past. *Classical* economics is basically making predictions by using measurements of what <u>has</u> happened. Gallup has created a system to measure what they call *behavioral* economics, which makes predictions based on their sense of well-being. What this amounts to is using intent as a means to predict how people will make decisions in the future based on how well they feel that their lot will be at that time. There are several things that comprise a sense of well-being: confidence, optimism, determination, creativity, hope, and drive. These just happen to be things that are reflective of a positive attitude as well.

So, the practical effect of this type of analysis is that businesses are better able to make plans about what they should be doing in the future. In other words, if they find a high sense of well-being, they will likely be more likely to produce more goods and be more innovative in their approach to the market. It is a liberating concept. Suppose the *classical* view reflects an economy that will be growing under the conditions that are in place at the present time. However, there are some things going on in the economy that cause people to not feel confident about the classical symptoms applying in the current situation. After all, perception is reality. One of the hardest things to do in business is to try to second-guess people.

I used to watch the *Nightly Business Report* on Public TV because you could pick up things about the economy in general by learning "tidbits" of what corporations were doing. Acquisitions, divestitures, and closings are certainly indicators in specific industries, but they may not be reflective of the economy as a whole. There are some that affect both industry and consumers. Things that affect industries that sell to consumers do for sure. Energy costs affect everything. One thing that affects corporations is the amount of cash that they have on hand. It's not the worst thing that can happen, but it may be an indicator of sales being less than normal. It's one thing to be playing the cash flow game of somehow coming up with funds to pay bills. It is entirely different to need your money working for you and, instead, sitting in a bank account. However, businesses may be holding on to their cash if they feel that sales are going to be down in the future. Of course, that is going to have a ripple effect.

This just makes a lot of sense to me because I always felt that operating a business by using accounting data was like driving by looking in the rear-view mirror. Economics is just a compilation of all the accounting data. While classical economics deals with this data on a rational basis, it can't account for the irrational way in which consumers think and act. That is where behavioral economics is able to offer a more accurate way of predicting.

Chapter questions:

- Reconsider the points made following the Special Apple Tree story. Keep these in mind as you read the rest of the book.
- Have you faced one or more of the *attitudes* that are described? How have you dealt with them?
- Do you agree with the importance of attitudes in approaching projects?
- Is it realistic to expect to overcome negative attitudes?

The Dignity of Profit

Part III:

What can we do about it?

CHAPTER 6

REVIVING COMMUNITY

To most people, the word "community" probably brings up thoughts of a place, a location where some number of people live. If you live in a very small place, the town or hamlet that you live in may be referred to as a community. If you live in a large city, your idea of community may be only a block or two. Many times, we think of the areas in a city or large town as having neighborhoods rather than communities. The size of the area will obviously vary, but some definable grouping determines how people connect with each other (or not!)

When I sold consulting contracts for retail businesses, my territory included New York City. When we consulted with a particular business, we would send a mailing out in a "spiral" pattern to a number of households that corresponded in some way to the amount of sales revenue that the store wanted to achieve through the sale. One of my first sales contracts was with a store in the Bronx. I was shocked at the small radius that 20,000 pieces of mail covered. Now, anyone that has been to that area knows that most of the residential buildings are very tall, so that would explain that phenomenon. The store owner was not surprised. In fact, he had purchased a store only a few blocks away that had been a competitor of his. He changed the format somewhat to offer some different items and services that his main store did not. When I asked him how he thought it was going to go for him to own such a similar store close by, he quickly told me that other stores had not been too much competition to his. He simply knew that each store served a particular "community," and there was a great loyalty to each. Now I am very aware of the sense of loyalty that can exist between customers and vendors, but this had more to do with how little mobility such large places offer. For instance, if you want to shop at another store for whatever reason, you will probably need to take public transportation to shop at that store.

A similar situation also exists in suburbia. Many downtown areas are virtually empty or getting that way. Therefore, people tend to shop in stores close to their homes if they provide the goods they purchase on a regular basis. I would refer to this situation as "location loyalty," and it doesn't seem to be the case for products known as "shopping goods." These are the types that people don't purchase without giving consideration to the various differences among these products: quality, brand, price, selection and the like.

So, here's what all of this about customers has to do with community. It has everything to do with it. For sure, a community is made up of different kinds of people. There is no such thing as homogeneity when it comes to a group of people. Even in an area like the Bronx, where people tend to congregate (live) in an area that has the same ethnicity, the interaction between the residents is not very strong. Restaurants, clothing stores, and the like gear themselves to the particular customer base, but that, in itself, doesn't create any sense of community. This is especially true when more than one particular type of business is located within the same confines.

This discourse is primarily intended to point out the importance of being a part of your community. There are many ways to do that, but being a person that people like is unfortunately not enough. You may be a member of the same church, be a regular participant in community activities/events, and be the kind of person people like to be around. These are all good things to do as a human being, and you can derive benefits from being a good citizen. I have been in that position, and I have known a lot of businesspeople who have as well.

SO, WHAT CAN BE DONE TO SUPPORT YOUR COMMUNITY THAT SHOWS YOU ARE CONCERNED ABOUT IT? ONE EXAMPLE IS

SPONSORING A COLLECTION DRIVE FOR FALLEN HEROES OR FAMILIES THAT ARE VICTIMS OF NATURAL DISASTERS.

If you have a business that sells items that might be important when during severe weather, having sufficient stock for those items when these events happen will endear you to your customers – especially if you don't gouge them. This can get out of hand, so don't go crazy. Selling tornado shelters can be a hard business to sustain, but having plenty of heaters on hand when very cold weather is predicted can be another means of community support. You can't manufacture loyalty; it is a two-way street. I've also referred to it as the absence of a viable alternative. On balance, being a good citizen is a good thing, but not everybody cares or remembers the good you did.

Once, I owned a hardware store in a town where a Boy's Club was being built. I donated all the paint for the project, and it was a substantial sum. Mind you I had been a member of the Chamber of Commerce and heavily involved with an arts organization. I had been an adult leader with my son's Boy Scout Troop and an officer in one of the larger civic clubs. Two of my children were born there. My wife was in a bridge club with several women who were influential members of the community and a very active member of a social organization. We were both very involved in our church as were our children. I've never been a social climber, and neither has my wife. Neither of us was from this place, but most of the people we were involved with were people we went to college with. With all of this involvement, you might think it would translate to our friends and acquaintances doing business with us at our store. Well, you would be wrong. Most of the women would have the temerity to talk about the ceiling fans they purchased in another town. There was no difference in brand or price for these fans, and the other town was 30 miles away! I even did my own TV commercials featuring the same brand of fans that they were driving out of town to purchase. My wife showed great restraint when these women would say, "I didn't know you sold ceiling fans."

Lest you think that I didn't know how to merchandize or something else, I spent far more on advertising than is normally recommended. We provided exemplary customer service, going far above what is called for. We offered pricing that was better than almost all of our competitors. We stocked items to support projects that our customers were involved in. We specially ordered from more sources than anyone else. Don't get me wrong, a lot of my problems had to do with a bad choice of partners. We did have loyal customers. It would have been a more successful venture if cash flow hadn't been such a problem. In the end, though, we experienced the success we had by being responsive to the needs of our customers and our community. I think things might not have gone as well as they did if we didn't have the involvement we did in the community at large. However, that was not the reason we were involved; it was because we believed in what we chose to do. I can never regret that. I've never been as involved in a community as I was there, and I have always missed those experiences. The people we helped were very appreciative – even if most of them were not our customers.

My experience in that community was mixed, to be sure. It included being seriously hampered by my relationship with a partner. It ended in a lawsuit against the bank that had "welcomed" our business when we sought a loan with my former partner. I mention this experience to point out that, along the way, I had to deal with relatives, friends, fellow members of a civic club, and people I had worked with on the arts foundation.

Bankers are very important to communities, but corporate interests get in the way of them being the vital part of the community they could and should be. I once knew a banker who funded a business out of his own pocket. The business became very successful, but it wasn't until years later that the banker told the owner. It's not the kind of thing that happens with bankers these days. That bank is now a large one with branches all over the state.

My experience with banks turned out to be typical of most banks today. There is a revolving door at many of the branches, and it is very hard to have any kind of relationship with a banker. Add to that, Wells Fargo, one of the nation's largest banks, was fined something close to $200 million for creating false accounts in the names of their customers. This is after the large banks were bailed out following the major collapse in 2007-2008. Very little was done to help bank customers with that bail-out!

Community members must look at how to work together to strengthen their community. Every part of their lives depends on it. Most people don't realize the significance of community because they are too focused on themselves. Schools, property values, and quality of life are all at stake. So are the safety and integrity of the citizens. I've seen the capital base become so eroded that people have to take major losses when they want to sell their homes. People don't want to buy because they know how hard it is to realize any sort of gain out of a sale when it comes time for them to relocate. Rental property loses value because the area attracts the wrong kind of renters. New housing is not built because the risk is just too high. There are programs available, but it takes a desire to get involved on more than just a personal level. It's not an easy process

Building Community

So, how do you build a sense of community if it is not by being involved in activities and supporting community events? To me, it is about being involved in the community as it relates to your business or organization. I mentioned in a previous paragraph that you should be responsive, and that has to be a very targeted effort. It also has to be for the right reasons – caring about making your community strong. It is a matter of being intentional in creating a sense of community with your customers.

Businesses that offer products that are craft- or construction-oriented sometimes offer classes that train their customers how to use their products. I have worked with quilting stores that have classes going on all the time. This may be about how to use a sewing machine that was purchased at the store or how to make something using a particular pattern. While the classes on using the machines are usually free to those who purchase them at the store, other classes offer discounts on supplies to help offset the cost of the class. The participants become a part of a club in some cases and socialize in homes or other locations while working together to create a project. These are certainly important to building *community*.

Not every business or organization lends itself to this approach, and in many cases, you are shooting at a moving target when you attempt to promote community involvement. This can be accomplished in other non-traditional ways. A business may not interact with any residents in the vicinity of their business. This is especially true if the primary location of the business is in a commercial area like an industrial park. There is no common ground, so to speak, for these situations. The business may have a trade organization that it belongs to. These groups are focused on doing what benefits their members. Beyond that, there is usually not something they have in common. Therefore, the community in that instance is not one that has a "moral" purpose.

On the other hand, a homebuilders' association is something that different businesses have in common with other businesses in the construction trades. There is almost always an association in most areas of any size. Developers can work with contractors and suppliers to create new housing projects and, as a consequence, seek to attract residents that will be living in a community setting. Some of these become true communities by having common areas for beautification and social gatherings. Neighborhood associations offer opportunities for cohesive groups to form, and these groups share responsibility for the maintenance of the common areas. Street parties and the like tend to be some of the ways that neighbors become a part of a community.

People who live in a community setting can take it upon themselves to weave businesses into their group. Many rural communities have few, if any, businesses. As the one where I now live, residents are not connected to each other except by family ties or geography. We sort of watch out for each other, but people who move in often don't have anything in common with the residents. I met my closest neighbor when his son failed to tend to a trash fire that spread to my property. He called the fire department and then came over to apologize. Fortunately, only some ground cover was burned, but that didn't form any type of relationship. We haven't spoken since (we just don't run into each other). I'm sure they would be glad to help if I needed it, but we don't share any common interests.

What has happened in some areas is that groups who have started a church or benevolent organization realize that something beyond housing and a food pantry is needed in their community. The best solution to providing the products and services that they need may be to attract entrepreneurs into the area. The best candidates for this come from those who have moved out of the area but still have ties to it. This process has been called "re-neighboring." It is not a simple endeavor, but it is a powerful way to help a community move from merely surviving to thriving.

What I have found is that the idea of attracting a small business to their community tends to just not turn up on the radar screen. Now, that is not entirely true to the extent that well-known restaurant chains like McDonald's, Sonic, Taco Bell, etc., will almost always be welcomed by the younger residents, including both adults and children. Of course, many of these franchises are not particularly interested in locating in low-traffic rural areas anyway. Start-up restaurants that aren't chains or franchises tend not to fare well. That is usually not the fault of the residents as much as it is poor planning on the part of the business owner.

My experience includes a start-up, a franchise-type business, a spin-off, and a couple of existing businesses that I purchased. All but the start-up had existing customers of some sort. As luck would have it, the start-up was the only one that had a truly local focus. It is easier to reach people locally as word-of-mouth is a powerful marketing tool – if it is positive. I built a solid customer base, but I am glad I didn't have to depend on friends. More on that later, but I mention it here to illustrate how important it is to work through people who are "coming home." However, that alone will not ensure success. That is why I believe community support is so important. Again, it's not easy, but if it were, everyone would be doing it. By the way, my start-up being a franchise-type situation may have helped me make it as much as any one thing. There was a recommended store layout, an opening inventory selection created for my geographic location, a private branding program, a national and local advertising program, and an annual rebate program.

The Need for Entrepreneurship

You might be wondering how possible it might be to find entrepreneurs who are Christians and who are interested in a start-up in an economically "depressed" location. That's a fair question, but the answer is less complicated than it might seem. I was given a book by Robert Logan and Tara Miller entitled *From Followers to Leaders* (Logan 2007, 13-24). They introduced an interesting notion that locating and/ or developing leaders from within the church is not the best approach in today's culture. It might not even be the right approach. I'm not, at this point, going to launch into an assault on how most churches go about conducting "business." I will say, though, that given the complexity of the tasks that churches deal with, developing leaders doesn't come naturally. As Logan and Miller point out, traditional paths to ministry are melting away as more and more denominations see a paradigm shift. While a forced shift, it is what they refer to as a biblical opportunity. This is one that leads back to early church methodology of an on-the-job, "in-the-moment" equipping style. Jesus used this approach to model the behavior that he wanted his disciples to adopt.

Of course, Logan and Miller are introducing what they believe is the approach that is called for in today's culture. This starts with recruiting people who are unchurched and may not even be believers. What I have seen of millennials tells me that the traditional church is in danger of becoming irrelevant. Churches do connect with their community, but most of these efforts are under the banner of "social entrepreneurship" (see Appendix J). Don't get me wrong, these are important endeavors. Where I have a problem with this approach is when they are not self-sustaining. This leads to rationing which, in turn, causes the creation of a business model that constantly deals with scarce resources.

Just in case you see my observations and solutions as being outside the purview of for-profit enterprises, let me clear that up right now. Luke 16 is a not-for-profit (NFP) organization. It is not, however, intended to only break even or constantly be seeking a hand-out for operations and projects. A NFP community event in my local area has been in operation for three years now. They only became an NFP after they had begun operations and were concerned about how they could keep from making a "profit." It wasn't the first time I had heard that concern from NFP's. To me, it makes perfect sense to do your best to operate without always having your hand out.

Funding Alternatives

This brings up another concern that arises from for-profit businesses who are asked to support NFP's. Many NFP's do not give enough concern to making sure their sponsors benefit from the events or ministries. At the same time, the officers of many of the NFP's are paid extravagant salaries. Oh, I get the argument about attracting good talent. Fundraisers are well paid, and that is a lot of what many of these officers spend their time doing. I have been on both sides of this, and I understand the need to avoid showing preference to businesses. Some NFP's have told me that they resist donations from certain businesses and organizations because of actual or perceived influence on the NFP. This gives the impression to outsiders that an agenda must be honored. A recent example of this is how donors responded to the Susan G. Koman Foundation choosing to withdraw its funding for Planned Parenthood. Koman had to reinstate its support to avoid losing major donor dollars.

No one gives money to a charity without expecting some sort of return. Many times, the return is not tangible, and here is where the "profit motive" comes into play. People give for a variety of reasons, and most don't expect the charity to be able to operate on its own. They will, however, make decisions about which charity they will support or how much they give. A Sunday School class I was in many years ago wanted to support some oppressed people in Africa. The government was run by a brutal dictator. While I wanted to support the people, I understood that the government was intercepting shipments coming into the country and holding them for ransom. My choice was to express my concern to the class. The outcome was that they decided not to send money to the ministry. I have second-guessed myself many times, but there have been many other cases where well-intended ministries have been unsuccessful in spite of many donations.

One situation I heard about was a missionary located in the highlands of Thailand. Like most missionaries, he had to become bi-vocational in order to continue in service. He had exploited the opportunity to market coffee produced in the area. The outcome was he made an arrangement with Starbucks Asia including a major investment in the project. This is a great example of how two problems were solved at once. I proposed such a situation for a ministry I was working with, but the politics within the support group caused it to be delayed until a long time after I was gone from it.

Natural Church Development (Schwarz 2006, 76-77) describes a way that those who supply funding to projects can be more involved to enhance the chance of success. A description of this is provided in Chapter 8 under the *Sustainability* section.

I started this section on "entrepreneurship" by describing how entrepreneurs while being the solution, are not received as warmly as is necessary to become a part of the solution. If people have a resistance to something new (which is quite common), it may take a while to accomplish much. The first step has to be to put together a group that sees the need and agrees with the approach. Even then, progress is slow.

Purpose Driven Life

Pastor Rick Warren (Warren 2002, 145-151) took on much of the Christian sector of religious America with his book by the same name as this section. It was a very thoughtful and honest look at how we have been "doing church" for many years. His chapter entitled *Cultivating Community* provided the following important points:

1. James 3:18 offers this: "You can develop a healthy, robust community that lives right with God and enjoy its results only if you do the hard work of getting along with each other, treating each other with dignity and honor." (Msg.)

2. Community requires commitment. It is only the Holy Spirit that can bring forth the fellowship that makes this happen, and this comes from cultivating it by using the choices and commitments we make.

3. People grow up in families that are not always blessed with healthy relationships. This means they may lack the relational skills to develop real fellowship with others.

4. Cultivating community takes honesty. Most people do not have anyone in their life that loves them enough to tell them

the truth. This makes for superficial relationships.

5. Cultivating community takes humility. Fellowships are destroyed very quickly by self-importance, smugness, and stubborn pride. Schwarz points out that Pride is at the root of all of the Seven Deadly Sins. We need to think ourselves less rather than thinking less of ourselves.

6. Cultivating community takes courtesy. Difficult people challenge us quite often when we try to maintain comity in our group. As hard as it may be to be courteous to these people, God has put them in our lives to show them Christian love.

7. Cultivating community takes confidentiality. The wartime saying "loose lips sink ships" also applies to communities. How can we attain true fellowship if we can't trust each other to hold information in confidence that would be hurtful to someone?

8. Community is built on conviction, not convenience. We need it for our spiritual health. It is not for us to just participate "when we feel like it."

9. Warren provides nine characteristics of a Biblical fellowship: sharing true fellowship (authenticity), encouraging each other (mutuality), supporting each other (sympathy), forgiving each other (mercy), speaking the truth in love (honesty), admitting our weaknesses (humility), respecting our differences (courtesy), avoiding gossiping (confidentiality), and making the group a priority (frequency).

Poverty and Community

Jesus said a lot about the poor. Here are a couple of the times he did:

"And when the disciples saw it (a woman pouring ointment on Jesus' head), they were indignant, saying, 'Why this waste? For this could have been sold for a large sum and given to the poor.' But Jesus, aware of this, said to them, 'Why do you trouble the woman? For she has done great work for Me. For you have the poor with you always, but Me you do not have always.'" Mt. 26:11 NKJV

"Jesus looked up and saw the rich putting their gifts into the offering box, and He saw a poor widow put in two small copper coins. And he said, 'Truly, I tell you, this poor widow has put in more than all of them. For they all contributed out of their abundance, but she out of her poverty put in all she had to live on.'" (Lk. 21:1-4).

In the Matthew passage, Jesus let His disciples know that their number one priority was to worship Him above all. They didn't know the "big picture;" the ointment was for a purpose that they didn't have knowledge of at that point – it was for His body prior to burial. While some of the "rank and file" disciples could be excused for their concern, John (12:4-6) says that the leader of this group was Judas. Jesus knew where he was coming from; Judas was being very hypocritical. This was not to let the disciples off the hook. It was just one of those instances that show the disciples were not fully on board with what Jesus was modeling for them.

JESUS WAS POINTING OUT IN THE LUKE PASSAGE THAT THE WIDOW'S OFFERING HAD BEEN SUPERIOR TO THE RICH PEOPLE BECAUSE OF THE SACRIFICE SHE WAS MAKING. THIS WOMAN HAD A DOUBLE WHAMMY; SHE WAS A WIDOW AND POOR TO BOOT.

I once was a member of a church where a member received $32 Million one year. Admittedly, this was not all cash – most of it was stock options. If he had tithed, the amount would have been double the entire church budget for that year. I don't know how much he actually gave; I'm pretty sure he didn't give ½ of a tithe since there were many who pledged substantial amounts that year. I don't know; I wouldn't care for him to donate to build something unless it was offset by a similar amount given to missions. Of course, it wasn't up to me, and that is a good thing. We Americans live in the wealthiest country in the world in terms of individual income. Those who give large amounts tend to want some sort of recognition for it. I even remember my dad talking about a visit with a woman in my home church when he was seeking pledges to the budget. My dad told her that a tithe was generally considered to be 10% of income. Her monthly income was

$86 (tells you how long ago that was), and her response was, "Oh, that's only 86 cents!" When my dad told her that it was $8.60, her attitude changed.

A church in the St. Louis area has a mission named Three Avocados. The name came from a story about a mission trip to Uganda. At the final worship service, a woman put three avocados in the collection plate because that was all she had. A businessman on the mission team began to look around for something that might be the genesis of a business opportunity to help this village. He found that the village grew coffee beans, and he started a company to import, roast, grind, and sell coffee under the name of Three Avocados. This church is also part of a worldwide eyeglass ministry to collect and redistribute glasses to the poor around the world.

There are lots of stories that illustrate how churches are helping needy people in a variety of ways. Unfortunately, the Three Avocados situation is all too rare. Most churches either give money to charitable causes or send members on mission trips. Virtually all of the charities have been checked out to verify that they are legitimate. Legitimacy doesn't necessarily mean they are really helping the poor in ways that would enable them to get out of the condition they are in without creating or perpetuating dependency.

Robert Lupton has spelled out in both of his books that the key to "moving the poverty needle" is a process he refers to as *gentrification with justice*. Many urban areas have seen declining communities attracting young families due to affordable housing costs because the land was purchased by developers at a low cost. This *gentrification* process has done a lot for upgrading neighborhoods while increasing property values. Adding *justice* to the process means that the neighborhoods help to move the needle when the poor are not just moved to another blighted area. It involves recruiting entrepreneurs to create businesses in the neighborhoods. It can also involve higher-income couples moving into the midst of some of the lower-income residents. It is a radical concept, but it has been done successfully.

In rural areas, this is easier in some respects but harder in others. Neighborhoods are not as distinct, but there are sections where lower-income housing prevails. Many "other side of the tracks" areas still exist. Still, replacing some of the housing with newer, higher-priced units can be a start to revitalization. In order to accomplish this, there has to be some subsidizing involved.

Toxic Charity

My life and ministry have been immensely impacted by a book by Robert Lupton with the same title as this section. Lupton has a great success story about his over 40-year ministry in an inner-city section of Atlanta. The book chronicles the arduous process of learning how to make a major change in an area that had long been plagued with chronic poverty. The solution involved creating a sense of community that ultimately permeated the area.

Here are some of the things Lupton learned that show how important it is to develop community relationships if you are attempting to change the lifestyles of the people you are working within a positive way:

Community Transformation

1. Transformation comes with a geographically-focused vision with measurable goals over extended time.

2. Key ingredients to have a viable community:

    Safety – a top priority

    Good schools

    Economic viability

3. Areas are not devoid of assets – there are abilities and a knowledge of history

    Listen to what they have to say about their situation

    Respect their opinions about the state/future of the area

    Look for a vision as to what solutions there might be

    Build partnerships with residents and groups that are willing to work on solutions and community development

Community Development Fundamentals

Further, in Toxic Charity (Lupton 2011, 138) we find some additional considerations:

1. There are specific stops in the process that need to be honored. In some respects, these "stops" are specific to a crisis, and Lupton points out that chronic poverty shouldn't be dealt with the same way as a crisis. I believe the main difference comes in moving from the first stop to the second one (or not):

   A. Relief – whether the situation is a crisis or a chronic problem, there are immediate steps to be taken to alleviate the suffering. Once alerted there are many kind-hearted souls who will come to their aid.

   B. Rehabilitation – at this juncture the object is to restore the victims to the state they were in before the cause of the problem they faced. It's easier to determine the extent of the help needed if it is a crisis. Chronic poverty generally doesn't happen overnight the way a tornado or some other natural disaster does.

   C. Development – as I said earlier, this is where the breakdown occurs. There are many people who don't see that it is their responsibility to help people to succeed. After all, but for whatever the reason might be, the victims wouldn't be better off than they are after stop B.

2. Resources are needed to proceed with C. because those who will respond to the need in may not find it in their hearts to go any farther. I'm not putting them down; everyone has limits as to what they can reasonably be expected to do. Whoever is willing and able to respond to the need of B. will do a great service, but the extent to which they are successful in restoring the victims to the state they were in before the crisis, it is not enough. OK, we are talking about restoring/rebuilding a house that can be accomplished in many cases, but what about restoration of lives? If this is a business, I don't know if even restoration can be achieved. My first thought about the devastation

3. Methodology – so, it is in the stagnant situation that is left after

relief efforts have been completed or at least been exhausted that efforts at community development must occur. I haven't painted a pretty picture because it isn't that at all. The following steps are what is necessary, but they are certainly not easy ones:

a. Focus on community – the singer Bono has done lots of work in trying to bring hope to debilitated areas, and he has found that you must focus first on creating a sense of community. It takes the following steps to actually happen, but we sometimes want to attack such problems from a broader perspective/approach.

b. Focus on assets – there are assets in most areas that can be exploited to begin the process of development. Use brainstorming activities to help ferret them out.

c. Focus on front-burner issues – there are things that cause some more significant issues to be subordinated. In Belleview, Missouri, the first thing on people's minds was some dilapidated buildings right in the center of town. As the survey conducted by the local United Methodist Church was being evaluated, it was found that people also wanted a place for children to play. The church bought the property, had the buildings demolished, and built a park which included a playground for the children. This is now a community investment that can initiate the growth steps. Now the need for businesses in the town can be considered as a way to help the town reach viability.

d. Focus on investing – look for ways to secure investments in the form of collateralized loans whenever possible. Grants should be used as incentives rather than charitable gifts with a "but for" requirement. That means that the grant should only be considered when a shortfall in available capital exists that can't be covered by a loan. However, it must enable the recipient to have a high likelihood of success.

e. Focus on leadership development – Local leaders are essential to helping to create and realize the vision of a successful community. They have to be the cheerleaders and champions of projects that are necessary for the dream to be realized.

f. Focus on pace – don't get ahead of the people. I have been guilty on many occasions of trying to draw the participants over the finish line. Remember the story about the five Boy Scouts in Chapter 5? Residents need to create ownership and become responsible for the outcome.

Natural Church Development (NCD) and Community

NCD is mentioned in various contexts in this book. There are areas used in the program by which a church is measured, known as the Eight Quality Characteristics (Schwarz 2006, 17-39). A survey is taken by a select group in a church, and the results will be measured against those of more than 70,000 churches around the world. The minimum factor (the quality characteristic with the lowest score) will be the area that is focused on initially. Holistic Small Groups are one of the areas it relate directly to *community*. Christian Schwarz, the founder of NCD, has written a number of books, and the one to address this factor deals with the reasons for a church committee or other small group is able to work together effectively.

Schwarz makes the case that what militates against a committee being able to function together goes back to the Seven Deadly Sins as designated by Gregory the Great (540-604). We aren't going to go in-depth as Schwarz uses several devices to assess and deal with each of the sins as they relate to community. It is enlightening, however, to look at each of the sins, the power behind that sin, and then how that power can be transformed into the quality characteristic that it relates to successfully.

The chart in Appendix A shows the impact of the Seven Deadly Sins on the process of developing *Community* by looking at how the negative force of the energies behind each sin can be redirected to achieve a positive outcome.

The point is that we typically deal with these sins in a manner that is counterproductive. All right, I'll admit that it seems a bit squishy to refer to being counterproductive in dealing with sins. That is precisely the point, however, in that there are two ways we usually deal with members who commit one or more of these sins:

1. The path of denial: this method seeks to ignore the sin. This path doesn't allow the possibility of transforming a negative into a positive.

2. The path of compromise: this views these sins as unavoidable. This seeks to justify sinful patterns or re-invent the Biblical definition of sin.

Doesn't it seem that redirecting sinful behavior toward acceptable outcomes would be a much better situation? This is not a simple matter of "flipping a switch;" most behaviors develop over time. Schwarz points out that the disruptive scenarios coming from sinful behavior need to be effectively dealt with if a sense of *community* is to develop.

Chapter questions:

- Do you agree that developing a sense of *community* is critical to the success of projects that seek to create economic viability in an area?

- Have you thought about *entrepreneurship* being a solution to community development problems?

- Do you believe that community efforts to alleviate poverty can be effective?

- After you read Appendix A, consider how impactful a positive approach to the Seven Deadly Sins can be in community development.

CHAPTER 7

LEADERSHIP

My coursework in college in the Business school was basically set up so that the introductory courses involved the basics of the particular discipline. In other words, Accounting 101 and 102 were introductions to accounting. It was more like bookkeeping, but it provided the basic knowledge that one needs to understand how the different income and expense items affected the enterprise. As one moved up the ladder in that discipline, the instruction began to include the elements of management for it. Depending on your major, you would possibly be exposed to various disciplines your major didn't specifically involve. For instance, if your major was Marketing, you would still be required to take some of the advanced Accounting courses. Also, courses that dealt with what we now call Human Resources were then called Personnel Management. Having management level courses in those two fields makes sense when you consider money and people are a part of every discipline as you practice it in the real world. Speaking of the "real world," the masters level courses were actually referred to as "managerial," and I found them to be quite different.

The reason I bring this up is there is quite a bit of difference between management and leadership. The college courses I spoke of prepared graduates to have the ability to make decisions from available information without getting too deep in the weeds. Most of the jobs I held as an officer in the Air Force were management types. Most jobs in government are designed so that people don't need to use judgment, for the most part. When I think about all the manuals we were required to adhere to, I am reminded of that fact. When there were inspections of the operations I was responsible for, we were mostly judged by how well we were "coloring within the lines." Leadership, as we think about it, was not a goal of a person who held a position within an organization in a support role. The person in charge was supposed to just make sure that the people under his/her command did their job "by the book." You weren't supposed to *think*. Everything was prescribed by the manuals, and people were judged on how well they performed the job as it was laid out there.

You may think it was a waste of time for me to go into the vagaries of being in the military. Please understand it is important to make the distinction between the practical effect of doing jobs like this in a bureaucracy and what real leadership entails. I was hired as General Manager for the company that brought me to St. Louis. When I was checking up on the company before accepting the position, I called some of their customers. One of them spoke of the problems the company had encountered with some of their people. My response was I didn't expect they wanted me to "stir the pot." At that point, I had owned a business and had faced most of the problems this company was having. When I told the president that he should have bought a tape recorder if he wanted someone to agree with him, he said he wanted what I brought to the job. As it turned out, what the president wanted was someone who would do what he wanted done. It's a long story, but leadership was not my job, although I had to take it on eventually.

Where I am going with this is leadership is a misunderstood endeavor.

RALPH NADER ONCE SAID: "I START WITH THE PREMISE THAT THE FUNCTION OF LEADERSHIP IS TO PRODUCE MORE LEADERS, NOT MORE FOLLOWERS." THE STORY OF THE *SPECIAL APPLE TREE* POINTS OUT THIS FACT BY ILLUSTRATING THE FUNCTION OF THE APPLE TREE (TO PRODUCE MORE TREES).

This is actually a rather new concept to me; I had always thought leaders were chosen to do a specific job. As Extreme Leadership Institute founder Steve Farber has said, "Your leadership is not about your position or title. It's about who you are, how you live and your ability to influence others to change things for the better -- at work and beyond." He explores that concept in his book *Greater Than Yourself: The Ultimate Lesson in True Leadership* (Farber 2009), where he discusses the true goal of leaders -- to build others up -- and outlines three keys to achieving this: expanding yourself, giving of yourself and replicating yourself. This stands in stark contrast to management which can be afflicted with "paralysis by analysis" in trying to make decisions about how to proceed.

Because of the dearth of leadership, I have observed in many places, especially in rural areas, I began to learn more about it. As an entrepreneur, I had to exercise leadership over the people who worked for me. Having created the businesses from scratch, it was up to me to provide guidance for the employees and to inspire them to do their best. Learning by doing is sometimes more beneficial than getting it through a lecture or something of that sort. My experiences have taught me to be observant and to keep learning. The problem with that is you have to be *doing* it while you are learning. I have come to reflect now that I am not "on the firing line" as I once was.

As a retail consultant, I learned to ask a lot of questions. Actually, you don't have to do that with business owners as much as it might seem. Most of them like to talk about their business, and you can find out a lot about people by asking many questions in some cases. The purpose of a consultant is to find out what is going on in a business so you can help them find ways to achieve their goals. I shared the statement earlier that people don't care how much you know until they know how much you care. Building a relationship with a client is an important key to helping them get where they want to go. Much of today's self-service economy doesn't provide many opportunities to build relationships with customers. If you are selling something to other businesses, you need to build relationships. The most important thing you can do in that regard is to try to understand the passion your client/customer has for their business.

A Christian View of Leadership

A lot is said about the importance of leadership, and much of it borders on inaccuracy. The reason we must address the importance in this setting is that Schwarz (creator of NCD) sees *character development* as a major precursor to *leadership development*. To ensure that communities and small groups are effectively led, we must have leaders with the character for it.

Through all the seminars and courses, I have endured, there's not much that really passes for good direction in developing effective leaders. The NCD approach (Schwarz 2006, 110-111) uses tests in some of the "courses" to assess modifications that are indicated. In addition, a Spiritual Gifts Assessment will guide Christians through a determination of where God has called them to live out their faith.

Dinesh D'Souza (D'souza 2008) wrote:

> Christianity enhanced the notion of political and social accountability by providing a new model: that of servant leadership. In ancient Greece and Rome no one would have dreamed of considering political leaders anyone's servants. The job of the leader was to lead. But Christ invented the notion that the way to lead is by serving the needs of others, especially those who are the neediest.

Much of what I can glean from books, articles, etc., regarding community development leads me to understand that part of the responsibility of community development (maybe the major part) is to bring all members along. This is not to suggest socialist principles are the way to go. I have known those who view the message of Acts, where the disciples had "everything in common" as advocating it. I haven't bought into that because there are no examples of that working for the entire community for the long haul. I lived through the 1960s as a spectator of hippie communes, and hierarchical structures took over after a relatively short period of time.

What we need here is for people to be effective leaders and to train leaders who will take over for them. When people are just out for themselves, society as a whole suffers. Community has to have a focus on avoiding "us vs. them." People have different motivations and lifestyles they are drawn to, and we are in danger of becoming a lot less than we can become if we succumb to a "lowest common denominator" mentality. Schools have struggled with this forever, it seems. It only makes sense to encourage all the members of a community to strive to achieve the maximum in the area of their calling. The parable of the "talents" illustrates we don't receive equal gifts. That doesn't mean we are unequal in God's eyes. The richness of our diversity gives us room to grow as believers.

Two different churches that I was a member of used a capital fundraising company to raise the money necessary to undertake major building projects. Their major theme was "Not equal gifts but equal sacrifice." That is a bit of a reverse of the "talents" parable, but it displays a fairness that we should all be able to live into. The importance of leadership in a community is to honor all gifts and to help all members to share in the responsibilities that being a member of a community involves. This is not just in monetary matters but in service as well. After all, money doesn't solve all problems, and it actually creates new ones in some cases.

The Need for Leadership in Communities

There really isn't the opportunity to choose those people who would make good leaders as much in smaller communities as in larger ones. This makes a lot of sense, of course, but the need is great in these areas. I have described in Chapter 5 on L.A.L.A. Land how people end up settling for things the way they are. You can add to that the resistance that folks in these areas have to working with others. The reasons are many, and it takes a bit of time and empathy to break through the shell that keeps these folks from accepting new ideas.

Communities are built on relationships, and leadership relies on relationships if it is to be effective. Leaders are best developed in communities/small groups. It is there that leaders can become "empowered" and they can pass that power on to others. Authenticity is important to being an effective leader, and it is easier to be that way when one is a part of a community. I noted earlier how it requires time to get to that point if you are an outsider. Once a person has learned that important trait, it can carry them as they move to another position. It should also be passed on to those who are being developed as leaders themselves.

Part of the problem that arises when people seek to characterize leaders is many times leadership is considered to be synonymous with success. For instance, success for Christian leaders is determined by the size of the group they are leading. Wealth and fame are also indicators of success in the minds of many people. The best leaders may never achieve the level of "success," as the world considers it. As described earlier, leaders are doing what they are best at when they are developing other leaders and getting them deployed.

The key to being effective at any task is to have good leadership directing, teaching, and empowering others. As I alluded to earlier, a large part of success in developing a sense of community is having the members relate to each other in positive ways. Leadership development needs character development, and this comes from being in an authentic community. The problem is people bring to a group all of what makes them who they are. The most commonly used term these days is *paradigm*. People naturally begin to become comfortable with how the world works when they feel they have learned enough to deal with life as they know it. The challenge comes when paradigms don't work well with each other. As unpopular as the notion may be, life is about trade-offs. We can't all have our way all the time. The sooner we recognize this fact, the better off we can be.

When Leadership Becomes Difficult

Some of the potholes that lie on the road to progress have already been presented. There will always be those matters that slow you down, but they don't have to be what sidetracks you. To me, the biggest challenge is getting around a person's attitude. Everyone needs to be working toward the same objective or progress will be hard to come by. Relationships will overcome a lot, but they can't do it all. Articulating the message you want everyone to understand is the starting point, but it can be misunderstood. After all, what you mean and what people understand it to mean can be two different things. Unrealistic expectations can be a major distraction as well. Everyone needs to be on the same page.

Limiting your span of control can help avoid some of the major issues that can seriously sidetrack your efforts. At some point, your organization/business will hopefully outgrow your initial structure. As you seek to expand, you will have new concerns: capacity, scaling your marketing, etc. More than anything else, your span of control will be tested. There have been many businesses I have encountered who have expanded, only to see major strains in the operation. It is easy to envision a multiple of your basic operations and sales increasing in the same proportion. It just doesn't usually work that way. One of the main reasons is the message you have worked so diligently to perfect will become diluted. Passion, relationships, and other key components will no longer be as effective as they have been.

Some of the most difficult situations arise when a bureaucracy is involved. Earlier, I mentioned the problems they can cause. This is because people tend to get all involved with their particular area to the exclusion of the organization as a whole. It is hard to convey the message clearly. Management guru Peter Drucker (Drucker) said that every person who works in an organization should have a pathway to the top. He went on to say there will probably need to be contractors for some areas (like janitorial, for instance) in order for this to be possible. The point is people need to see a way for them to grow within the company. That will help them be interested in the mission of the company/organization.

Jesus (John 10:10-18) pointed out the difference between how the "shepherd" treats his "sheep" and how a "hired hand" treats them. It doesn't seem likely Jesus was saying that He was the only one that cared about the "sheep." Evidently, Jesus was referring to how He cares for his followers compared to some of the religious leaders who were in it for the money. If we are talking about a business, it is going to be a fact that the owner will care more about it than those who just work there. If it is a volunteer organization, people answer to a higher power. However, most volunteer organizations have people who are paid – some of them quite well. The sincerity and dedication of the paid staff are almost always considered to be questioned as opposed to people who care enough about the mission to work there for nothing.

Jesus told his disciples when he sent them out in pairs: "Don't hesitate to accept hospitality, because those who work deserve their pay." (Luke 10:7). People must pay more attention to this verse than they do to the one about *hirelings*. If you have ever offered to do something for people without charging, you may have found they are sometimes suspicious of you. They must feel you have some sort of an angle and will get something out of it anyway. The bad part about such situations is they don't always say the words to you that reveal their skepticism about your motives. Of course, there are some who expect you to do things for them at no cost to them. I guess the problem is most people just think about themselves and view everything through the eyes of that selfish motivation.

Being a leader suggests power is somehow vested with that person. The problem arises when the leader tries to retain the power for their own benefit or uses it to control others. Christian Schwarz (Schwarz 2012, 14-17) points out that leaders are to be *empowering* rather than just *empowered.* Author Jim Collins says that leaders should tap into the "genius of a thousand helpers." When leaders empower others to become leaders themselves, the collective intelligence creates a synergistic power that far exceeds what a single individual can exert.

One of the challenges in understanding what leadership is has to do with defining success. People who have achieved wealth and fame are usually characterized as good leaders. They may be, but it is not because of wealth and fame. Elsewhere I have written about the difficulty of actually defining what success is. I used the acrostic S.U.C.C.E.S.S. as the name of the valley where the things we consider to be true success reside. Of course, all of this is relative to the situation. I once heard the greatest disappointment in life is when you have climbed to the top of the ladder only to find it was leaning against the wrong building.

So, the major point here is leadership is much more than power. It has a lot to do with capturing a vision and being able to gather the people and resources around you to be able to see that vision to fruition. Rev. Michael E. Williams (Williams 2017, 40-41points out that: "If we cannot imagine a better world, we have neither the vision nor the motivation to work toward it." However, just having the vision will not do it. Just being a good manager will probably not get you to that point. You must be able to communicate it clearly to others and convince them to aid in the effort to reach that goal.

There are two other appendices that continue the idea of being successful at leadership. These have to do with communication and intentionality. If you cannot communicate your vision effectively and then demonstrate you are intentional about seeing it to fruition, it is going to be difficult for you to be successful.

Chapter questions:

- What has been your experience dealing with *leadership* issues?
- How do you feel about the notion that we generally select leaders the wrong way?
- Do you see the need for real leadership in communities compared to what exists?
- Do you agree that leadership and vision must go hand-in-hand?

THE DIGNITY OF PROFIT

Part IV:
What is the Payoff?

CHAPTER 8

S. U. C. C. E. S. S. VALLEY

If you have made it this far in the book, you will now get a look at what awaits you at the end of the journey. It does not mean the work is done. On the contrary, the work is now beginning – at least the physical part. However, a major step has been taken that got you out of L.A.L.A. Land. You might have lost track of what was accomplished there. Maybe you got bogged in the details. Hopefully, you didn't think you could skip that process and try to take the "Express Lane." No matter what you do in life – if it is worth doing – there are no shortcuts. The importance of any journey is learning from the process. If you don't, you will find yourself very disappointed. This comes from my own experience; the cost has been dear.

Winston Churchill once said, "Success is walking from failure to failure with no loss of enthusiasm." Perseverance is one of the prices we pay to make it to success, but as I wrote in Chapter 2, it helps to know what success looks like. It also helps to be flexible and adjust to the inevitable potholes lying on the road to success. That is actually a great metaphor in that we don't turn around and go back home if we hit a pothole while driving. That is unless you break an axle or knock your wheels out of alignment.

To keep this journey metaphor going, we could look at some of the other mishaps along the path. I don't want to beat this to death, but probably one of the major difficulties we face has to do with the nefarious characters lurking out there. When I was in the Air Force in

New Mexico, there was an incident involving three different "service stations." They really were that because these were stations that actually worked on cars as well as selling gas then. Anyway, the stations were lined up along the main highway through town. The trick these station owners came up with was spraying silicone on the alternators of cars that stopped in to get gas. The gasoline was pumped by station employees, and they usually checked the oil level, etc. at the same time. The "extra" service was to spray the alternators while they were at it. The cars were then able to make it to the station located in between the other two. All of them split the proceeds from this "trick."

My experience in my current location involved a few of these "tricks." They weren't all intentional; some people just think they are qualified to do any kind of work. It's sort of the bane of living in a rural area. I have been told people who live in the city are stupid. It wasn't clear how they came up with that, especially given all that had to be redone thanks to their ineptitude. All of this has made me wary, but I believe in helping people get over their sense of dependency or misguided self-sufficiency.

I have enjoyed using acrostics in this book because they always help me to sum up a number of thoughts in one word. One example I use consistently is "A.C.T.S." This was given to me a long time ago for use in prayer. It stands for (A)doration (C)onfession (T)hanksgiving (S) upplication. These are certainly important to be included in prayer, and I think they are in the proper order.

Anyway, the ones used here have come to me in the wee hours of the morning on nights when I was unable to get back to sleep. Some of my best ideas have come to me that way. I believe the Holy Spirit communicates with me in that way. It fits me very well in that I tend to overthink matters I am struggling with. It's a trust thing. I've subscribed to the notion that "all things come to those who wait – as long as they work hard while they wait."

DON'T GET ME WRONG: WE SHOULD WORK AT WHATEVER WE ARE CALLED TO DO. IT'S JUST GOD WANTING US TO TRUST HIM, AND WORRYING IS A SIGN THAT WE DON'T. TO ME, IT IS A PART OF

THE MINDSET THAT HAS TO CHANGE IN ORDER TO BE ABLE TO BE A REAL CITIZEN OF SUCCESS VALLEY.

So, let's look at what it takes to be a part of this community. I use this word because it is where we will be going next – exploring how to form a community. You see, moving from L.A.L.A. Land to S.U.C.C.E.S.S. Valley is probably going to involve getting the residents to come together so that progress can be made.

Here's the acrostic:

(S)tandards

(U)nwavering determination

(C)haracter

(C)ooperation

(E)nthusiasm

(S)elf-sufficiency

(S)ustainability

Standards

The short definition of standards is a level of quality or attainment. It may seem a little odd to be making a point about standards when most of this book is about taking a risk by doing things differently than they have been traditionally done. The point is a "rut" is not a standard. Things don't have to be done exactly the same way for there to be a standard; they just need to have a consistent level of quality. I'm not sure how you make any progress unless you have guidelines to keep you on track.

Suppose there is no standard octane for grades of gasoline. You pull up to the pump to fill your car, and you see the different grades listed as "regular," "high test," and "super." With no octane rating or any other measure to connect to the grades, you have to take the word of the refiner that there is a difference between the grades. How likely are you to purchase that brand of gasoline? The fact is, without certification of some sort, you cannot have any confidence in there being any real difference.

My thinking on the importance of *standards* is that doing something new, different, and significant must be judged by what is considered to be the standard. Taking our gasoline example, we might want to come up with a different fuel or mixture that got higher mileage for the same price or cost less for the same mileage. If we use octane as the standard, we can judge the value of the new fuel/mixture. There are other considerations, of course. For example, exhaust emissions could be a target for keeping mileage "standard" while lowering them. Perhaps there could be an attempt at increasing mileage above the "standard" without increasing the price. Once again, one can't judge the real value of these innovations without *the standards* of existing products or services.

Integrity needs to be a part of the process of determining and maintaining standards. The importance of this goes to whether or not you can trust people who make claims about what they provide. Probably the most important impact on American consumers and innovators is whether foreign imports are held to the standards of U.S. producers. A manufacturing company I owned made webbing tie-down cargo straps. One Chinese competitor offered a strap having all the right sizes and features of a strap the industry rated at 10,000 # breaking strength. However, they did not list a strength rating. We had one tested, and it was significantly below the standard for a comparable U.S. product. Of course, Chinese factories are not very accessible for inspectors to visit, and a lot of product makes it into the U.S. without being tested or certified.

Communities must have standards as well. Please don't get the idea I am suggesting discrimination. Laws prevent us from being unrealistic in what we expect or will tolerate from residents. When you consider L.A.L.A. Land and the loose manner that people live their lives, there is a difference that matters. There needs to be an awareness of how the community and its businesses are viewed. This is especially true in areas where an expectation of selling to those who live outside of the community exists.

Unwavering Determination

Another way to think about this term is persistence or perseverance. I've shared the story about the man God told in a dream to push on the rock in Chapter 1. We have to be discerning and to be certain we are hearing clearly from God that this is what you are truly called to be. We will discuss ways to do this in another section. Having done that, you should be "all in."

Passion is an amazing emotion. It can lead you through adventures you may never have imagined you would encounter. However, without the discernment mentioned above, a momentary burst of passion may adversely affect your life – perhaps forever. If you are "all in," there are limitless possibilities. Many people give up too soon, and they carry that burden for a long time.

A caveat is in order. There are times when you need to be able to "read the tea leaves" to make sure you are on the right track. You must be careful when you make the decision so you avoid spending a lot of your life on the wrong path. It is also important to ensure you don't mistake "speed bumps" for "dead ends." There are also detours you need to take along the way. I have learned my pushing ahead sometimes gets ahead of God's timetable. When I think I have seemingly "hit the wall," God provides new energy when the time is right.

St. Augustine had a quote I hold onto: "Trust the past to God's mercy; trust the present to God's love; and trust the future to God's providence." He always knows better than I do. The important thing is to never give up on God; He never gives up on you.

Character

Much of what happens in life dictates that character is vitally important commodity. When dealing with people who have become calloused and numb to life, the only thing that can cut through the thickness of their shell is being of strong character. This doesn't mean you have to be perfect – only Jesus Christ can claim that. In fact, being transparent can be the most important quality you possess as a leader.

Character has been described as what you do when no one is

watching. That's not bad. We are as real as we can ever be when we aren't even trying to fool God. OK, that's a little scary, I know, but people who think they can fool God have issues we can't deal with as humans anyway. That is unless psychiatric help is involved.

Another way to think about *character* is a set of traits acquired over time and mostly through experience. Many parents teach their children the "Golden Rule": "Do unto others as you would have them do unto you." (Matt. 7:12). It is important to note that Jesus did not say: "Do unto others as they do unto you." That would suggest that retribution is OK. In its purest form, the Golden Rule covers a lot of territory. What do you do you wouldn't want people to do to you?

Personally, I can't stand for people lying to me. Maybe I'm not in the majority, but I don't think people like being lied to. It is poor character, however, to feel like lying is OK to support a position you hold onto without having solid ground to stand on. It's not a crime for candidates and their supporters to lie during a political campaign. Oh, I don't know. Shouldn't there be something wrong with that? I also think it is wrong to lie to yourself. If you do, why wouldn't you lie to others? I'm pretty sure it is poor character either way,

Some want to say character is in the eye of the beholder. It may be so with respect to differences in cultures. However, within a culture itself, a character may have "nuances" that cause people to disagree. Social justice is a term that gets bantered around these days. When different *standards* come into play, characters may take on different meanings. If you feel your group (whatever that means) has been denied opportunities other groups have, you may think of the people in the other group as not having good character. I have found many people in more rural areas who feel that folks from cities don't have much common sense, but they also feel the city folk are just out to cheat the ignorant *yokels*. Thus, they feel city folk have bad character. Consequently, the city folk have to prove a negative, which is very hard to do. It places a particular challenge on folks from cities that would actually like to help them.

Like standards, character is developed over time. What you are early in life will change, one way or the other. Shakespeare wrote: "To thine own self be true...." People can see through you if you are not real. One of the proudest moments in my working life came when I decided to drop in on a prospective customer in a school system. I had not met the man before, but he allowed me to share what I was selling for almost an hour. He said he didn't have any money that he could spend on the system I was offering. He went on to say he would be very interested if he did because he believed I would not try to sell him something he didn't need. To make this even more meaningful, he said he was on his way home for the day when I came in. I guess people can say anything to try to "let me down softly," but this has happened on enough occasions. I believe I can tell when someone is doing that.

The point is, in a sense, character is all you really have, that is, "you." I guard closely the reputation I have built. I have my flaws – we all do. Being *real* is extremely important in achieving true success. A saying I can remember from long ago is: "Who you speak so loudly I can't hear what you are saying." My parents instilled in me the importance of "remembering who I am." Oh, I know they were referring to my heritage, but I realized it was up to me to carry on. It was clear to me that what I would become would either be a positive reflection on my ancestors or a negative one. In the end, people will judge me for who I am, so it is up to me to build my character. If my heritage is not as I would want it to be, who I am can largely overcome or confirm it. It's up to me – and you!

Cooperation

One of the first pieces of social behavior "advice" we give children is to share. When I was in elementary school, report cards had a grade for "deportment." I was a reasonably bright kid, but it took me a while to get what that was all about. When I did, I wondered if they didn't tell us what it meant because it was really for our parents. I'm not sure if they even grade it these days. After all, we wouldn't want to offend anyone. Seriously, we have gotten to the point where we don't want to be judgmental. Supposedly, this is to show how sensitive and open-minded we are. Going out on a limb here – I know this is judgmental – but it seems we don't want to be judged ourselves, so we put up with things we just shouldn't endure.

There was a report I remember from several years ago that told of a change in what the most familiar Bible verse was. It used to be John 3:16. We all know that one, but the newer generation chose Matt. 7:1 – "Do not judge, or you too, will be judged." What Jesus was telling us here was to avoid hypocritical and self-righteous judging, not judging behavior with discernment. This is not intended to be hurtful but constructive. In that way, we can exhibit a cooperative attitude to remove obstacles to community.

Jim Clifton, Chairman of the Gallup Organization, makes a big point about the need for the U.S. to make partnerships around the world in *The Coming Jobs War* (Clifton 2011, 165). He feels that these partnerships will cause us to think more seriously about cooperation in a way that helps increase the well-being of many people. Clifton uses Gallup's research to point to the difference that exists today with regard to making predictions about the economy. He makes an excellent point about using *behavioral economics* rather than *classical economics* (see Chapter 5). His case for determining and addressing what helps create a feeling of well-being is compelling. This also supports the saying I shared earlier: "People don't care how much you know until they know how much you care." This is also the way that Natural Church Development approaches outreach to the un-churched by the quality characteristic of *Need-oriented Evangelism* (Schwarz 2006, 36-37).

The point I am making here is without cooperation, not a lot is going to get done in the way of making disciples or helping people to do for themselves. It took a lot of experience with mission trips before I understood that. Billions of dollars are spent every year by well-intended people going to places where the residents are perfectly willing to let you do for them – many of them who don't lift a finger to assist in the work being done for them. As cynical as this may be, it is a major impediment to cooperation. I mean, it takes two to cooperate. Of course, you could argue that not rejecting your efforts might qualify as cooperating. That's just too obtuse for me, and I can't agree. If you have experienced this, there are a lot of us who could tell stories that would set your hair on fire.

The partnerships that Clifton is talking about go beyond cooperation. For a long time, certain industries have operated *cooperatives.* When I was in the 4-H Club eons ago, one of the projects was learning about cooperatives that were formed between farmers. The most common ones were rather general in nature. The way they worked was by farmers basically banding together to form a business in which most of the customers were also stockholders. The risk of the business was shared by all of the stockholders, and they also shared in the profits (assuming there were some). Some of those are still around, but many other types have cropped up. Many electric "co-ops" are covering rural areas in America today.

The Rainbow Network, an organization that focuses on helping the economy of the people of Nicaragua, has an interesting co-op involving banking, businesses, housing, and education. In their case, every member of the co-op is responsible for the success of all of the others.

The retail hardware industry has several co-ops and virtually every independent retailer belongs to one or more. Virtually all independent hardware wholesalers are members of buying groups, which are essentially co-ops. These co-ops have branding at the retail level as well. This is in the form of signage and/or private-branded products. Being a part of these co-ops generally affords significant price advantages and national advertising.

There are many advantages to cooperation – formal and informal. "Playing well with others" makes life a lot better than the alternative. Businesses seek partnerships with each other and with their customers, and that has many advantages. The key to making this work is ensuring each party understands what they bring to the union. Some indefinite promises will not do it. It is amazing how quickly a party can forget or "misremember" one or more parts of such a promise. I once had an agreement with a person who was sewing webbing on cargo straps where the materials were shipped directly to him. What was supposed to be on hand never matched reality. When I tried to put our agreement in writing, he was incensed and refused to sign it. My only recourse was to terminate the agreement. I later hired the person who was doing much of the sewing on our products, and she told me several things he was doing, including stealing some of my products.

No matter how you cut it, partnerships are hard to pull off. I believe Clifton is dreaming when he feels we can make a large number of partnerships around the globe. Just look at the ones we have (and had), and you will see there are too many factors militating against long-term partnerships. In 2016, Great Britain voted to withdraw from the European Union. It was primarily over totally free movement between the member countries – open immigration, if you want to call it what it really is. Just look at how divided the American people are over immigration and several other matters. Our experience has shown us that contracts are made to be broken; you only need to look at the divorce rate in this country.

So, is it possible to have cooperation? The answer is: you can to a point. Wherever possible, cooperative agreements should be in writing. You must realize change is going to come. Parties to the agreement come and go, and when disagreements arise, lawyers can become involved. In the end, however, cooperation is important to being successful.

Enthusiasm

Passion is one of the synonyms for *enthusiasm*. Being passionate about something is probably going to make you enthusiastic. If you are not enthusiastic about what you are doing, it is really hard to get others on board with it. I was on a plane once with a young man who had just started working for a pharmaceutical company. He proudly told me that the last four letters in *enthusiasm* stood for "I am sold myself." Of course, that's not true, but it makes a good point. In my sales position, it is very difficult to sell something you don't believe in.

Enthusiasm is contagious. Don't get me wrong, you can't fake it or be overbearing with it. Enthusiasm should come from the excitement about what you can do for your customer or client, not what they can do for you. There again, it is important for relationships to be balanced so one side isn't at a disadvantage. When that is the case, the disadvantaged party is going to eventually tire of the arrangement.

The process for a person to become enthusiastic about their product or service is just that: a "process." First, you need to have an understanding of what your customers or clients are looking for to solve their problems. Determining what the problem is and how to fix it is a good way to endear yourself to the customer/client. Knowing you have solved their problem and that it will be beneficial to you should make you enthusiastic about serving them.

Being enthusiastic yourself is just the beginning. You have to have a customer/client that is enthusiastic as well. If you have done a good job of solving their problem, you have a good start at getting them "on board." Don't be surprised if the excitement you anticipate doesn't materialize. Believe it or not, people will sometimes give you a task like solving a problem just to get rid of you. Just as unbelievable is some salespeople don't follow through.

I alluded to this earlier, but you can be overly enthusiastic. This tends to turn people off, so just because you get excited, don't go overboard. People usually get this early in life, but I offer this as remedial advice if nothing else. I have found it better to share your findings on a piecemeal basis so the prospect can stay with you as you unveil the solution. OK, some people take more to "get it" than others, but you will catch on as you get experience.

Remember, you are a part of a team bringing a positive message to people, and they will be more likely to welcome you if you are enthusiastic about what you are telling them. If you don't have a solution, make sure they are aware of your intention to keep trying to solve the problem or at least lessen the severity of it.

Another "e" word that could fit here is *encouragement*. The Apostle Paul wrote to the Thessalonians: "Therefore, encourage one other and build each other up." (1 Thes. 5:11 NIV). It is one of the most important things Christians can do for other believers. Life is generally uphill, and we need to remember who made us and cares for us. We face a lot of opposition to what we are doing on this earth. If we are true to our calling, most people don't care about it. Many people you are trying to help won't care why you are there or how you get your encouragement. It is important to continue to be enthusiastic and encouraging to those you work with.

Self-Sufficiency

One of the major problems one encounters when working with charitable entities is them becoming dependent on the servants who come in initially and those who return to help keep the project going.

119

Mission projects tend to find recipients willing to avoid doing anything to help themselves in the absence of team members. This is not only frustrating for the team, but it is not helping move recipients to become capable of helping themselves.

This is where some teams miss the point of being in service to those in need. It was mentioned earlier that Robert Lupton makes the point that we most often treat chronic situations as if they were a crises. A crisis calls for immediate action to bring the situation back to where it was before the crisis happened. When the crisis is a large one, like a tornado or hurricane, there is usually a tremendous turnout of folks coming to help. With all that help it is tempting to keep on going farther. This is called for sometimes, but it is also possible to create a sense of dependency if you are not careful.

Chronic situations take a long time to develop, and they will take a long time to change. There is usually some underlying reason the situation has become chronic. It may be that a factory closed, or land was claimed for an airport expansion or whatever. People have become displaced by events beyond their control. Depending on how the response affected the residents, remediating the situation may call for drastic measures. I have been involved in such scenarios, and residents have learned how to adjust to the conditions they are in. Unfortunately, government programs have created such a safety net they aren't really interested in doing much, if anything, to better themselves.

The real problem with the situation we face in much of rural and inner-city America is a culture is in such a high state of dependency that it is almost beyond chronic. In many cases, it has become a two- and even three-generation condition. That makes it very hard to break into. When I said that once, the person I was speaking with said: "But if you can break into it, it will make a big difference." It's the thought that keeps me going, and I hope it will be for you as well. The future of America depends on people working and producing and making our economy strong. Clifton makes a compelling case for getting as many people back to work as possible.

I realize that facing the prospect of being self-sufficient can be a bit scary. My wife and I both graduated from college in August, and I didn't go on active duty in the Air Force until November. That wasn't a problem because we alternately stayed with our respective parents. We had saved enough money from jobs we had in college to take care of our incidentals, so we were fine until I started getting a regular paycheck. For the longest time, even though I changed jobs several times, there was essentially no gap in income. However, beginning with starting my own business, I found out what it was like to have an irregular income stream. Then, it vacillated from regular to irregular for the rest of my working life. My wife had jobs at times with a regular paycheck, but she also had her periods of irregular income as well.

The important point here is no one was "carrying my water;" I was *self-sufficient* (OK, my wife was helping). Working on full commission is not for everyone, and neither is being your own boss. The reality is either of these scenarios is quite gratifying and can be very financially rewarding. Nonetheless, business ventures are never fully supported by any outside entity. There are contracts and long-term agreements which can provide sufficient income for a time. However, there is always uncertainty in business, but it doesn't mean you should avoid living your dream. If your dream is meant to be, you should prepare for it by doing your research and preparing yourself for those speed bumps that will inevitably come.

With regard to working with a community to develop a successful business model, remember you are doing it for the development of the local economy. Where self-sufficiency comes into play is making sure you are not creating a situation where the community is heading for trouble. You will likely be using funding and labor provided by the community at large and/or funds from grants. However, it plays out no good comes from launching the venture only to have it founder because of a lack of sufficient funding.

Sustainability

Self-sufficiency is critical for a venture to operate without constantly "having its hand out." Historically, most non-profit enterprises have relied on donors. That makes the situation of no direct benefit to the donor. In such cases, the manager has to be concerned about raising funds and having a successful project as well. If you have achieved self-sufficiency, you can focus on the success of the venture, which will take care of both objectives.

Christian Schwarz, NCD founder (see Chapter 6), lists six *growth forces* (Schwarz 2006, 65-86) that can determine the ability of a church to become healthy. One of them is *sustainability*, and he contrasts the two main ways that organizations receive charitable funding. As I noted above, the funds given by the *donor* model only flow one way from the donor to the recipient. A focus on the acquisition of funds becomes more important than the outcomes achieved from the funding. The more logical (and productive) model is the *cyclical* one. In this instance, the beneficiaries contribute to the financing of the enterprise. As Schwarz puts it: "The energy has come full circle. The same energy that is spent working on the project provides its financial backing."

Certainly, sustainability depends on adequate funding, and you don't want to be focused on your bank account balance all the time. The reality is there are certain matters you should certainly be focused on as well. I share these because this is, in the end, a business we are operating.

Market – no business venture is going to remain viable without a market. In fact, you can't even get into business if you don't have customers/clients. How you keep them is the challenge and the major key to sustainability.

Cash flow – people who haven't been in business for themselves usually think you need to have a lot of cash in the bank all the time. In some instances, this might be a good idea. However, mostly, you need to have your money working for you. Sustainability requires managing your cash flow judiciously.

Management – most ventures fail due to poor management. While you can't control all of the surprises that pop up in the life of a business, preparation will allow you to work your way through. Experience is the only effective way to prepare, but you can't make all the mistakes that may occur. Training can help, but seeking the wise counsel of those with the necessary experience can make a tremendous difference between success and failure.

People – some operations can be run by one person, but when that one person is unable to work or to continue in the business, it grinds to a halt. I have been in that position for a while now, but I have retirement funds to help sustain me. When I was a sales rep, I had to be on the job essentially 24/7. At least one of the folks I worked for did not find it in his heart to accept a lapse of activity on the part of any of the sales force. Fortunately, I was able to make it, and I am thankful for that.

Supply of materials – If you are making something, you need supplies and materials to do so. This would include food preparation. It's hard to offer lemon meringue pie if you don't have some of the necessary ingredients. I have found it very helpful to have a backup supplier of the materials needed to operate. Suppliers go out of business, find a customer they would rather sell to than you, and sometimes change their terms to make it no longer economically feasible for you to do business with them. You also need suppliers who will "go the extra mile" in those instances when you have an immediate need.

None of the items listed above will take care of themselves. A lot of what I have written has to do with making good relationships. Having competent people working to get these items done will do a lot to make your venture sustainable.

Probably, the most important thing you can focus on to help sustain your venture is your attitude. Perseverance can keep you moving toward the long-term goals you need to attain sustainability. You will, of course, need it all along the way. Setting and meeting *standards*, maintaining *unwavering determination*, exhibiting *character*, achieving *cooperation*, becoming *enthusiastic*, learning to be *self-sufficient*, and, of course, arriving at *sustainability* are the ways you become successful.

Perseverance alone will not get you to your goals, and you will need to address problems as they arise. A lot is involved, but you will only succeed if you work your way through them. If you are willing to *persevere*, your chances of succeeding will be greatly enhanced. If things don't work out for whatever reason, you will be able to rest assured that you did all you could.

"Successful and unsuccessful people do not vary greatly in their abilities. They vary in their desires to reach their potential." --John Maxwell

Chapter questions:

- The *success* described in the acronym is the result of making the changes that have been suggested in the previous chapters. Do you see the connection?

- Of course, there are other factors – perseverance, vision, and the others mentioned in the book. Can you think of some others?

CHAPTER 9

MOVING FORWARD

In this final chapter, we will look forward to how the information provided in this book can impact the problem of poverty and lack of meaningful work for Americans. I will also bring into focus the important points to remember/consider when determining how to make a meaningful difference in many lives.

S.U.C.C.E.S.S. Valley is still just a part of the journey; it is not a destination. It is a metaphor for life in many ways because everything we do becomes the story of our lives. Just because you have arrived in the Valley, it doesn't mean that everything is in a completed state. The trip to the Valley has helped you to learn what it takes to be successful, but surprise, not everyone is on the same page. Just because you have all the pieces to the puzzle doesn't mean the puzzle has been put together or that it has been put together correctly.

In the initial stages of your arrival in the Valley, you must build relationships first and then develop them into a team. There are a lot of people who provide various ways of team building; some work better than others. However, there are various roles to be filled on your team based on the nature of the project. If you have done a Spiritual Gifts Assessment, you have made a major step toward getting yourself focused. A community-building activity would be very beneficial as well. The last thing you need is to have discord within your group.

When you begin to engage the residents, there are some matters you need to consider at the outset. You can do what is known as a S.W.O.T. Analysis. "S" is for *strengths,* "W" is for *weaknesses,* "O" is for *opportunities,* and "T" is for *threats.* It is quite enlightening when you lay these things out. By doing this, you can determine the particular items that will either benefit your project or stand in the way of progress. Not all of them can be overcome completely, but at least you will be able to know how to deal with them.

All of the components of S.U.C.C.E.S.S. require refining continually. It may seem that you shouldn't try to fix something that isn't broken. The reality is that stuff breaks all the time; you just don't know sometimes. Tweaking is extremely important to avoid breakdowns in the process and to keep your project in step with any innovations that will enhance success going forward. With all of that, you will still have occasions when things go wrong. This is when you get to put the S.U.C.C.E.S.S. components into action to rebuild the process.

As an example, Standards will be updated (hopefully) as the process works, and new challenges will push your team to strengthen the expectations you have for the participants. Outside variables are always acting on your system, so you have to change to in order to react appropriately. There are some that are inevitable: costs fluctuate; supply of materials, etc., will change; people move; tastes change; new regulations are enacted; and natural disasters occur. That list is not exhaustive, but you get the point.

Probably the most important thing leaders can do is to create a process to train their replacements. There are lots of reasons for this as well. How leaders are chosen makes for an interesting study. Most of the time, the process is rather unscientific. Experience in leadership positions is usually a major factor. This can result in replaying old movies, so to speak. Leadership is dynamic as well. A lot of this was dealt with in Chapter 7.

From much of the research I did to give backup for my thoughts and recommendations, I found a couple of areas that warrant attention. To me, these seem to be possible solutions to some of the major struggles we face now and in the future.

The Importance of Developing Young Entrepreneurs

There are a lot of issues we deal with in today's economy, and the one that should give us the most concern is getting more Americans to work. Regardless of what the Gross Domestic Product (GDP) might be, the one that reaches into the heart of every family is the matter of how income is going to be provided for the household to pay bills and plan for the future. A lot is said on a regular basis about the rate of unemployment, but the reality is much more than that.

If the percentage of people working is in the high 90s, it really doesn't matter to the person who is unemployed. As far as they are concerned, the employment rate is 0%. As dire as it is to not be included in the percentage itself, looking at the bleak prospects for getting a job can be even more demoralizing. A lot of what has been presented in this book has to do with helping people be able to be engaged in meaningful work and providing for their families. Government programs abound directed at helping people prepare themselves for employment. Some of these are well-intended but miss the mark. Connecting people with available jobs is a challenge. So-called "safety net" programs seek to provide assistance to those who are "in between jobs." Unfortunately, many people have learned how to "game the system," so they do quite well even though they are not employed.

David Smick (Smick 2017, viii) points out that the real salvation for the U.S. economy will come from Main Street Capitalism, which is the Great Equalizer. At the heart of the problem we face in our economy is the fact no solution lies with the government, corporations, or the "central" banks. These groups are the reason trickle-down" economics somehow doesn't make it to the main street level in our country.

Men Without Work (Eberstadt 2016, 18-31) points out several disturbing statistics, but the one at the top for me was the fact there are 10 million American men of prime working age, healthy and capable of working, that aren't working and are not even looking for a job. These aren't counted in the unemployed ranks, and there are others not counted as well. Eberstadt calculates that the real percentage, including all categories, is approximately 28%. When all the costs incurred by this large number of unemployed people could be totaled, my guess is it would be staggering. Add the "cash economy," where people are paid for work that never makes it to the tax-reporting system, and the real total would reflect a major drain on our economic system.

Starting Early

Stephen Covey, author and consultant, tells of an experience he had in Germany with two cab drivers: "One was an older gentleman, and the other was a young man. The older cab driver was longing for the old days. As he drove us around Berlin, he described the awfulness of all this so-called 'new freedom' and how he now has much less opportunity. The younger cab driver looked at the same exact world, and yet he was excited about the opportunities. He was thinking creatively about how he might improve his condition. The other was trying to maintain the old position." Winston Churchill is famous for saying, "If you are not a liberal when you are 20, you have no heart. If you are not a conservative when you are 40, you have no brain." (Churchill 2014). Agree or not, the reality is the world/life catches up with you when you get older. Covey's little story shows how this conservativism can make us overly cautious. It seems to me the concept of *learned helplessness* comes into play. I address this in Appendix H. It takes time for people to get to that point; younger people haven't travelled that road yet.

Smick recommends some actions we should take to activate the support of the young at very early stages:

1. Set up an investment account for every child at birth. This would make them stockholding capitalists at the earliest level.

2. Create a system to identify and find the next generation of superstars. This would include directing private enterprise capital to be available to them.

3. Encourage new enterprises and support them incrementally.

My wife and I actually set up an insurance policy when our children were born, and it would be great if parents or grandparents would see fit to help children at the earliest possible time to get involved. This is actually a good way to fund a college education if that is in the cards. There are other investments with some of the same advantages. It has always amazed me how investments climb so steeply when they are kept to a mature stage.

Schools Are Where the Future Entrepreneurs Are

Jim Clifton provided a lot of information about students in his book, *The Coming Jobs War* (Clifton 2011, 131-139). There are currently more than 75 million students enrolled in schools in the U.S. There are nearly 50 million in the fifth through twelfth grades. These are the ones who need to replace the business leaders of today. Unfortunately, 30% of those students will drop out or fail to graduate on schedule. About 50% of minorities are dropping out. Currently, there are approximately 100 million people working in the U.S. Part of Clifton's analysis shows the future doesn't look good for the U.S. based on the drop-out rate. That is not the only thing concerning me. Where will the jobs come from for the ones who don't drop out? So, to me, the problem is a double-edged sword. If there aren't jobs, the economy is going to be strained further. This also means the U.S. is not going to be the factor in the world economy it has been.

MANY SCHOOLS ARE NOT PREPARING STUDENTS TO BE COMPETITIVE ON THE WORLD STAGE. THE BLAME CAN BE SPREAD AROUND: DROP-OUT STRATEGIES HAVE BEEN INEFFECTIVE; TEACHERS' UNIONS DON'T FOCUS ON A QUALITY EDUCATIONAL PRODUCT; BROKEN FAMILIES AND LOUSY PARENTING. IN THE END, A LOT OF MONEY IS BEING SPENT, AND MANY ARE WONDERING WHAT WE ARE GETTING FOR IT.

Very little is actually being directed toward preparing our young learners to create businesses at the level where the greatest impact can be made.

Vocational programs have never really sought to address local market needs unless they make some sort of arrangement with particular industries to help them prepare workers for their needs. From what I can determine, programs schools participate in to lead to proficiency in a particular trade are, for the most part, created in response to a grant or other funding that seeks to meet a need that may exist regionally or nationally. One of the local school systems has trained a lot of welders who are being bused 50 miles each way daily where there is a need for their skill. They also are training sign-makers to start their own businesses when the market is shrinking in all areas due to internet sellers.

Robert Lupton has spent over forty years in Atlanta working among low-income residents. He has made major inroads into changing how charity is being done there and elsewhere. From this experience, he has found that everyone, even 6-year-old children, has an innate desire to make a difference. He believes this is why young people sign up for mission trips. Because of this, those who put these trips together market to youth. Unfortunately, much of what goes on during these trips is make-work activity. In the end, lifting people out of poverty does not end up being the focus of their efforts.

Lupton has really hit the mark with *Charity Detox* (Lupton 2015) when he contends the solution is to create entrepreneurial ventures in neighborhoods like the one he has worked in for most of his life. What he is advocating is a "ground up" approach as opposed to one coming from a program or initiative that works its way down to the folks who need it most. Nonprofits alone will never move a community out of poverty. Many of the programs available to those in need tend to miss the mark or actually induce people to be unproductive. Only wealth creators can provide the type of assistance that will make a difference. Many examples of this are provided throughout the book.

The action arm of Luke 16 Corp. at this point is R.E.A.C.T. This stands for Recruiting Entrepreneurs to Assist Communities to Thrive. Notice I said "thrive," not just "survive." You may know the praise song with the title (Thrive) that makes this point. There is a big difference. This area is surviving, although just barely in some ways. It needs to be able to THRIVE so survival doesn't turn into something worse. Lupton states that only entrepreneurs can make this happen. Most programs are only focused on individuals – such as education, welfare, and job training. We have all of that now, and it's not working. Entrepreneurs invest in the community, create jobs, attract money to the area, pay and collect taxes, and get involved in community activities. No program or project can move the poverty needle beyond a small amount. Christian entrepreneurs behave in ways that benefit communities beyond the things stated above. Helping weave the principles Christians are supposed to live by into the fabric of area citizens can help to build community.

Addressing the Challenge

The Coming Jobs War (Clifton 2011, 49-61) addresses the matter of making predictions about the economy's future in a different manner than what has been used for a very long time – traditional economics, he calls it. This is where predictions are made based on historical data. What he recommends is what he calls Behavioral Economics. The Gallup organization has apparently invested a lot in this endeavor and believes it will be appropriate for a very long time. Part of it probably has to do with the fact that it is forward-looking and will not be affected by new situations coming along to change what has happened in the past. This process is designed to focus on the sense of well-being people have. By using it, marketers can seek to address what is currently going on with people.

What follows is basically what Clifton has to say about using this methodology in making a difference at early stages with school-age youth. Leadership strategies will have to focus on the cause rather than the effects of hopelessness. They must be built on hope rather than grades and attendance. Increasing hope isn't easy, but it can be done. It must be done on a local, citywide basis rather than on a national one. Leaders must:

1. Focus all local groups on student engagement or the confidence to graduate. Gallup has found the most important factor in student engagement is the teacher. Parents, teachers and mentors must understand hope is more important than the mechanics of math. The payoff for a student should be a job, not graduation. Even better, they should have an exciting career.

2. Use Gallup's pro bono Student Poll as the core behavioral economic metric. Administer it every spring and every fall in every school in your city with every student. This needs to involve every student in the 5th through 12th grades. The software surveys children and records their state of mind. This

can help to keep the student's hope candle lit because, when it goes out, it is nearly impossible to relight. (see below)

3. Reduce by half the number of students with no hope of graduating. Doing this will fix your dropout problem because you put it on the road to correction.

4. Involve all the local social-based organizations. Have a big kick-off meeting. Involve as many organizations as you can that have an impact on youth: Operation HOPE, American's Promise Alliance, The Y, National 4-H Council, Girl Scouts, Junior Achievement, and others. Seek how each of them can have an impact on student confidence and how they can align their forces to double it.

5. Double student hope. The groups listed above have always had great people with super-powerful missions and purpose, and they have more answers than anyone else. Every youth needs a mentor.

6. **Super Mentors** – These are the ones who can guide, advise, encourage, & mentor small business to success. They can be almost anyone, but they are not entrepreneurs or innovators. They are the ones who light the fires under the entrepreneurs and innovators. They are willing to take a risk for an individual or an idea. The assistance they give is an essential part of creating new jobs.

The rationale is spelled out pretty well in these excerpts, and I believe the emphasis on youth is well-placed. As I wrote earlier, young minds are more open to opportunities. Planting the seeds early on in a person's life can produce fruit later. In order to bring this into a meaningful endeavor, the *Super Mentor* concept is absolutely critical. Not only does this facilitate the training and innovative activity required, it gives the components of community interest and guidance. **My experience has convinced me that without a sense of community spirit and enthusiasm, young innovators and entrepreneurs will go elsewhere.** There are many factors supporting a fertile breeding ground for the ideas that will drive development.

Another suggestion Smick makes doesn't directly affect youth, but it is important for local communities to consider and hopefully enact.

These can be young adults or others who have an interest in improving their employment potential. In some locations, parents and children attend evening classes (at separate levels):

Fund Adult Tech Education – Strengthen the community college system by supporting adult evening programs with grants that update IT and Internet-related skills.

With the potential existing for strengthening the community college system, it seems there should be a way to partner with people who would like to take an early shot at assisting students to explore where they want to spend their working lives. While most who are knowledgeable will rightfully contend this is too late for many, different age groups need to have separate handling. The major point is some adults are limited in their formal educational experience, and this has proved to be successful in some situations. At a minimum, there can hopefully be more exposure to opportunities that can open new worlds to young people.

A New Kind of Incubator

Traditionally, incubators have been very strict in the way they work with start-up businesses. As a consequence, many entrepreneurs are excluded. Specifically, they content (or require) a limited time period by which the business should "graduate" out. Retail businesses would not work at all in these instances. Some businesses are not ready to graduate, but they are still allowed to stay in many incubators. These very sharply defined situations are really not working well for the most part. Most of them close or end up being perpetual landlords for the same businesses year after year.

The "new" type is more of a *virtual* incubator. This means they are not location-specific. There's nothing prohibiting incubators from being in the same location as other businesses that are not incubated. When you consider that this opens the possibilities traditional incubators do not, it makes a lot of sense for other types of businesses – like retail. After all, if the object is to help businesses to become self-sufficient, why isn't it OK to let them stay in one location and receive help for a period of time appropriate for that business?

Of course, the notion that guided a lot of the thinking for

traditional incubators was that a central reception area be provided, but there should also include a conference room and office equipment to be shared by tenants. Some incubators certainly operate that way, but being able to open the door to others makes it a very good idea to avoid the shortcomings prohibiting it. Good, solid mentoring is needed to make sure a start-up business is successful. This means services formerly available to tenants are not nearly as important as enabling business owners to receive the assistance they need.

Another concept is to have a non-profit select a potential owner/operator to conduct a "hands-on" incubating scenario. A team of entrepreneur coaches will guide the person(s) chosen in the early stages of the business's life. The *incubation* period of the business would depend on a number of factors. Each situation is different, and there has to be dedication on the part of all parties to make the project work. These would probably work best in the traditional setting, but they need to be flexible enough to accommodate the uncertainty of a business. Investment by the *coached* owner would need to fit the needs of the business and the suitability of the owner. Again, flexibility is the key to making this work.

When incubators have been set up in the past, they follow the same concept as stated above, but they basically rely on standard ownership scenarios. It is anticipated that a community environment will greatly aid in being successful. Also, careful recruiting and vetting of potential owners will be another very important part. This is not a "slam-dunk" process, but the outcome can be very satisfying when it enables relationships to develop to bring the community together.

Avoiding Insurmountable Challenges

Much of what has been presented in this book has attempted to overcome the hurdles preventing communities from growing in all ways that help them function as they should. Business is an important part of a community in order to enable residents to learn how to support one another. Sometimes, residents spend their money outside of the community and then expect local businesses to support schools and the activities a community wants to have. Many rural communities are struggling to survive in today's culture because businesses have left or closed and not been replaced.

Jay Walker, a founder of Priceline, said the reason the U.S. has been so successful as a place for start-up businesses is it allows people to fail. (Walker 2016) It is commonly known we learn a lot more from failure than from success. If you think about it, learning from failure is a lesson we don't wish for. The irony is that we can't afford to miss the experience. Dolly Parton once said she wouldn't take anything for the experiences she has had, but she wouldn't give anything to have them over again. A lot is packed in that statement.

L.A.L.A. Land is undoubtedly the major impediment to being able to help change the landscape in depressed areas. Most of the rest lifted up in this book has to do with ways to change your own mindset (if necessary) or to encourage you to get involved, knowing there are some areas where you can make a difference. **I once heard it said that one of the hardest things to do is to get other people to do what you want them to do. That applies even if what you want is the best for them.** This country is still the land of opportunity, albeit that it is harder to achieve than in some times past. We need to realize we are standing on the shoulders of giants – those who sacrificed so we could have those opportunities. However, the sense of entitlement is pervasive in the U.S. and stands directly in the way of making the kind of progress called for.

There is no "magic bullet" that will kill off the effects of L.A.L.A. Land. As was mentioned in Chapter 5, that covered this, any one of the conditions is enough to sidetrack the process. When you have multiple issues present (which is often the case), the task is very difficult. It can be done, though; others have done it. What is required is a determination to stay the course.

Ultimately, the answer is to create a genuine attitude of *community*. Remember, a "rising tide lifts all boats," but the boats must be in the water (to keep the metaphor going). If you look around the area and see able-bodied adults (mainly men) sitting on their porch watching the world go by, you know the job is going to be a tough one. What this really means is these people have been left behind by fate or by choice. Everyone needs to be a part of the solution. After all, the mindset focused on someone else providing you with the wherewithal to exist will keep a person in the *Land.* I don't think a lot of time should be spent on where the blame lies except to try to overcome the barriers they create. There are certainly plenty of them, but what passes for social justice today is a side issue in many cases. If a healthy community can be achieved, the strength that comes with progress can result.

Go For It!

Marvin Newell gives a definition of the *Great Commission* (Newell 2010, 16) that works for our purposes:

The task given by Jesus to the Church through the disciples that authorizes it to carry the gospel everywhere so that all peoples might have the opportunity to believe in Christ as their Savior and become life-long followers of Him.

While Matthew 28:18-20 (cited elsewhere) is most commonly connected with the title, *Great Commission*, there are others. Check these out if you want to see how they support the best-known passage: Mark 16:15, Luke 24:44-49, John 20:21, and Acts 1:8. The keywords in these passages (not all the same) support the *Commission* given in Matthew. They are 'go,' witnesses, and sending. These are action words and tell us we are not expected to be passive in this endeavor. Newell gives a description of how evangelism plays into this, even if it is not expressly stated in these passages:

The process of communicating the Gospel of Jesus Christ in culturally sensitive ways so that all peoples everywhere might have the opportunity to repent of their sins and place their faith in the redemptive work of Jesus for the salvation of their souls.

In Appendix H, we discuss communication and look at how it can be verbal and non-verbal. *Going* is non-verbal, but it speaks volumes to the people you are seeking to serve. OK, not everyone will be excited if you are there, and that is why relationships are so important. In a real sense, communication is only one-way unless there is a working relationship with folks in the area where you are striving to create *community.* Witnessing can be verbal or non-verbal. What I am suggesting is that you use both methods to help people to learn more about why you are doing this:

1. People need to know you are doing this because Jesus told you to – the Great Commission.

2. You have a gift you are to live into, as we all do. You will be helping those you came to serve learn what their gift is and how it is important to being all God called you to be.

3. Building relationships and creating community is a part of the mandate Jesus has placed on all of us.

4. Most of all, you need to communicate that it is the love of Jesus you know and you want others to know.

If these are not what motivates you, you might want to consider their importance before you commit yourself to this mission. Being genuine is extremely important in communicating the message the mission involves. Regardless of whether you are involved in a traditional "mission trip" (repairing houses or doing Vacation Bible School) or a mission involving changing people's lives by impacting their ability to care for themselves, those you are serving must know you are there for the right reasons. One of the problems with the way mission trips have been conducted in the past is they don't deal with the heart of the problem: a sense of entitlement and despair. If we simply give them something they should be able to do for themselves, we are communicating to them we don't value them in that way. What it says is we don't care about their **dignity** as a human being, and this is not the message Jesus wants to share.

In the Preface, I shared how I felt about *evangelism* once upon a time. I also shared how I changed when I came to understand the NCD concept of *Need-oriented Evangelism* (see Chapter 8). It was not long before I discovered that one of my Spiritual gifts is *discernment*. The way NCD views the area of evangelism is that there are those who have the gift, but we are all to practice it. In other words, when we are reaching people where their needs exist, we are practicing evangelism. In my case – and possibly in yours – my gift of discernment enabled me to view the situation of mission trips as a well-intended enterprise that misses the mark. To be an effective member of the Christian community of believers, we are to use our gifts to serve Jesus. So, let's take this to its next logical step. An effective community will have representation from all of the spiritual gift areas. If we all have the

Great Commission as our directive, our gifts should be used to support it. There is something all of us can do, and hopefully, this book has given you a sense of how you do it.

Here are the steps I recommend:

1. Pray for God's guidance for you in living up to the Great Commission.

2. Review what the book says about the importance of taking on the task of revitalizing communities.

3. Take the plunge by building relationships with like-minded believers.

4. Encourage others to take a Spiritual Gifts assessment so each member of your group/community will be able to find the part they should play.

5. If your target is your own area, you should begin to conduct a survey and do an assessment of the area to try to determine the process to help your area form a community. The book should have provided you with some important assistance in this regard. There are others cited in this book.

6. Keep praying and keep learning.

My Wish for You

At the risk of being somewhat repetitious, let me say many years of experience led me to write this. It is intended to be a guidebook of sorts for those who want to be engaged in a mission but haven't been sure about it. If your hesitation has been you weren't sure mission activities "hit the mark," if you didn't feel you have anything to offer in the way of discipling others for Christ, or if you had reservations about business and faith working together, it is my sincere desire this book has helped you see we all can be involved and hopefully engaged in the process.

Please visit the website for Luke 16 Corp: www.luke16.org. There, you can get a sense of the vision we have for bringing into balance the three main areas of life: Physical, Creative, and Spiritual. It is important to understand that, without these three areas being in balance, we can't live life to the fullest as Christians.

We spend an inordinate amount of time with the *Physical* part, where we focus on the *things* of our lives – sometimes to the exclusion of most of the other two parts. Luke 16 focuses on the other two: Creative (self-expression) and *Spiritual* (relationships). Both of these are integral in the process of being able to revitalize communities. Transferring the energies involved in these from acquiring things as we do in the *Physical* area helps us to be in the service of Jesus Christ rather than for ourselves.

Hopefully, you picked up on the idea that *Real Profit* is about healthy relationships – relationships that help form community. As challenging as the process is, it is worth the effort. Passion drives vision, and vision points to the location on the roadmap where we need to be in order to be successful. That success means that you have achieved *Real Profit*.

Chapter questions:

- Look around you. What is the situation in your community or project area like with regard to involving youth at the earliest possible time?

- Start to consider whether any of the examples or suggestions would help you to be successful. Where can you start today?

- Are you up for the challenge?

THE DIGNITY OF PROFIT

APPENDIXES

APPENDIX A

Seven Deadly Sins

ENERGY	SIN	BIBLICAL MODEL	REDIRECTION OF ENERGIES	QUALITY CHARACTERISTIC
Power	Pride	Request of James and John Mark 10:35-45	Greatness through servant-hood	Empowering leadership
Pleasure	Gluttony	The believer's freedom 1 Corinthians 10:23-33	What is beneficial?	Effective structures
Identity	Envy	One body, many parts 1 Corinthians 12:14-27	Everybody is needed	Gift-based ministry
Sustenance	Greed	Feeding the five thousand Mark 6:32-44	Multiplication through giving	Need-oriented evangelism
Justice	Anger	Clearing the Temple of John 2:13-17	Zeal for God's cause	Loving relationship
Renewal	Sloth	Rest for the weary Matthew 11:28-30	Finding rest by taking the yoke	Passionate spirituality
Intimacy	Lust	Anointing by a sinful woman Luke 7:36-39	Relating affection to Jesus	Inspiring worship

APPENDIX B

Profit and Capital

It is important to understand the relationship between profit and capital. First of all, capital is required to make a profit. Capital takes many forms, but like it or not, it is the engine that drives any economy. Profits are required to maintain or increase capital. An investment of capital will become extinguished if there is no profit involved.

The definition of capital is "the wealth, whether in money or property, owned or employed in business by an individual, firm, corporation, etc."

OK, "So what?" may be your response, but it is important to understand these basic facts before we can adequately address the importance of the relationship. Capital takes a lot of forms: monetary, human (labor), intellectual, moral, and maybe some others you can think of. Even moral capital can be used up - just like the others - by failing to employ it properly. Some would argue, and perhaps they are correct. Before I deal with that, it makes sense to look at all types of capital in relation to profit.

Monetary (Financial) Capital

This is the most obvious item to fall under the "capital umbrella." We are all familiar with *capital investments, working capital, high-risk capital, fixed capital, capital stock, capital interest, etc.* When a business is starting out, capital can be essentially the "seed corn." Just in case you aren't familiar with the term, seed corn refers to corn that is used as seed to start the next crop. Another "so what?" Well, as simple as this concept is, people don't seem to understand it sometimes. There was a song in the 1960s, I think, that spoke of wandering in the desert and coming across a water pump and bottle of water. The point of the song was that the "finder" could drink the water and move on or use it to prime the pump. Priming the pump was the only option, allowing the bottle to be refilled for the next person. If I remember correctly, the refrain was that you have to "have faith and believe."

According to the definition above, capital is wealth. It goes on to state that it is "owned or employed." If wealth is simply owned, I would contend that it isn't actually capital. Some businesses may be using wealth as a means to increase its worth as an investment. In the consideration that we are using here, either way it is designed to produce a profit. Some people feel it is safer to hold onto their capital in case they have to buy back stock (if they are a publicly traded company). This is one of the reasons that I believe Jesus, at least in part, was referring to money/wealth in the parable of the Talents. (Matthew 25:14-30) When the decision is left up to the financial department of a business, sometimes decisions are made on the basis of safety. Thank God for them because they keep those of us who can get over-exuberant in line. Some people feel the return would be better in the stock market or some other investment than in funding a business. That is actually true in some cases, but normally, cash-in-the-bank is the bane of most businesses. The reason is capital needs to be working, not sitting idle in the bank.

Once again, if there is profit, the reason is capital employed to do so. Of course, investing capital and employing it in the pursuit of profit is not guaranteed. What is guaranteed is if you don't have the opportunity that capital affords, you won't have a profit. This is certainly true regardless of whatever kind of capital is being employed.

Perhaps the definition of "business" is in order at this point. Here's one:

> An organizational entity involved in the provision of goods and services to consumers. Businesses as a form of economic activity are prevalent in capitalist economies, where most of them are privately owned and provide goods and services to customers in exchange for other goods and services or money. Businesses may also be social non-profit enterprises or state-owned public enterprises charged by governments with specific social and economic objectives.

The difference between for-profit and non-profit enterprises is not necessarily what most people think about them. For-profits are pretty easy to understand – make a profit or go out of business. I have known of businesses and actually worked for one that amazing stayed in business for many years without making a profit. The reason is obvious: the new capital came from somewhere. I became pretty good at managing *working capital*, but that can only get you a little way down the road. Investments or loans are the most common ways to get new capital to keep a business afloat. Many people who own businesses won't recognize the problem of "putting good money after bad."

Non-profits are used to avoid paying taxes in many cases. This is pretty short-sighted, but some get away with it. I have had my moments with the IRS, and I strongly suggest giving such a plan a lot of thought. Then you should choose not to try it. Other non-profits see themselves as organizations that get grants and donations and spend them on worthwhile projects. That type of organization is probably the most common.

So, what is the role of financial capital in a non-profit? For the most part, it is used to fund projects of some sort. Unfortunately, not all are really legitimate. I remember a case on the *People's Court* where this guy had a non-profit to run a mushroom sighting business or something like that. He was just paying himself for doing something he liked to do. I don't know how things like that get through, but I guess it's not worth spending time trying to sort it out. Legitimate non-profits employ capital to essentially give it away or maintain a platform to do so. Capital is necessarily replenished on a regular basis from some source(s), or they go out of business.

Let me say at this point that Luke 16 Corp was created to be a different kind of non-profit. It's not unique, but there aren't many that operate the way it does. The design is that it is a conduit to get money into the hands of homeowners or entrepreneurs to create opportunities to own their own homes or start/purchase their own businesses. Grants flow through and do not fund the operation of Luke 16. Building houses for sale or creating businesses to turn over to individuals are the primary objectives/activities of the corporation. The only reason for the non-profit status is to be able to qualify for the grants available. Otherwise, the corporation is self-sustaining. The business plan provides for the sale of houses and the sale of businesses that have been incubated in order to create businesses that can operate on their own.

Human (Labor) Capital

In some ways, it is inappropriate to refer to people as human capital. Over the years, I have learned of several different ways of referring to people who work in a company: personnel, assets, and human resources. It's my choice to consider workers as capital. Certainly, it is depersonalizing to refer to people as assets, and it is perhaps the same for capital. I don't think I would like it too much, but I am not considering them in this way except that I want to honor the value they offer to the business.

Too often, business owners consider workers as *things* rather than people. Marcus Lemonis is the host of *The Profit* TV show (CNBC). One of the three points he looks at when considering whether or not to invest in a business is *people*. As I have watched many episodes of *The Profit*, I have noticed he looks very strongly at the value employees are contributing to helping the business stay alive. He also has little patience with those that are not. While some businesses don't require employees, many do. Even those who don't may have a partner or investor they have to deal with. The relationship between the one who "calls the shots" and the one(s) who do most or all of the work is critical. Absentee owners have to be concerned about the loyalty and dedication of the workers.

In looking at how to treat employees when they are considered capital, it seems it is much the same as any type of capital. Remember, capital is not to be left in an idle state, it is not to be "used up," and it is to be replenished as necessary. I happen to be one of those folks who hates employees wasting time – time that I am paying for. The opposite is to push people to the extremes to get the most out of them for what you are paying. The best answer usually is to *replenish* to avoid having them become lazy or burned out. Replenishment can be time off, additional training, some sort of appreciation for a job well done, or perhaps a pay increase. Your particular situation will dictate the course of action you should take.

One further consideration is a little delicate to discuss. It deals with key-person protection. This usually means getting a special life insurance policy to cover the loss of an employee due to their death. This should be set up as a benefit to the employee if they leave. I worked for a family-owned business where one of the family members had the company purchase policies on certain employees. He kept the coverage in effect after they left the company. It was felt that they, for whatever reason, were likely to die within a fairly short period of time. All of them outlived the company that was sold out of bankruptcy meaning the money was completely wasted.

Intellectual Capital

This is a situation involving training or experience or where a person has created something trademarked, patented, or copywritten due to their design or development. These may be critical to your business, and you certainly need to protect your interests. Again, this type of capital will probably need to be refreshed or otherwise improved in order to retain or increase its value. This is not an inconsequential matter; it can be the difference between surviving and thriving or going under.

Scientists of any type, as well as engineers, can very likely be the source of formula or computer programming that is the heart of the business. Protecting your interests can take different forms, and all of them may be necessary. At a minimum, insurance protection should be secured. This can be on the formula or code itself, and it can be on the life of the creator. Trademarks and patents belong to the creator sometimes, and I'm not sure about protection unless you have an employment agreement signed by the creator before coming to work for you. Non-compete clauses in an agreement involving employment have not withstood legal challenges due to the restriction of a person's ability to make a living for themselves. Just know that you should seek legal assistance before you get into any situation that might put your investment in jeopardy.

Moral Capital

Most people would not consider *moral capital* as something to be considered as capital at all. To my way of thinking, there aren't many organizations effectively operating without a moral compass. This is especially true if it is dealing directly with the public. In Chapter 6, I speak of becoming a part of the community you are in. The nature of the community may differ greatly between different types of businesses. It's hard to become a part of the community if you are not dealing with people on an ethical basis. Again, this is all over the place, depending on lots of factors, but some are pretty basic.

I once heard a story about a butcher somewhere in Europe during the Middle Ages who had been holding his thumb on the scales in order to cheat his customers. When the customers found out about it, they put the butcher in the town square inside a cage. Eventually, the birds picked at him until he died. Now, we are a bit more civilized these days. People tend to complain on internet sites or just stop patronizing the business. None of these techniques lead to desirable situations, but I personally prefer the modern ways. Of course, those who seek legal remedies for being cheated can do a lot of damage to your business.

Preservation of Capital

Jesus addressed the notion of not allowing capital to lay idle when he told the *Parable of the Talents* (Matthew 25:14-30). In the case of the two who got a return on the "investment" that the manager made with them, there was clearly a gain or "profit" realized on their transactions. The one who didn't make a gain/profit was punished for not having anything to show for the experience – except he did hold on to the principal. The outcome for him shows how Jesus felt about people not producing *fruit*. We are clearly called to produce fruit; Jesus gave us an example of how he responded to the fig tree that was barren.

Matthew 21:18-19 relates a time when Jesus was hungry and approached a fig tree that only had leaves on it and no fruit. He cursed the tree, and it died. The disciples marveled at this for several reasons, and we probably do as well. It would be easy to characterize this as another example of Jesus' becoming frustrated as He seemingly did with the moneychangers at the Temple (Matt. 21:12-13). Dr. John MacArthur explains the significance of this by pointing out that the fig tree is often used as a symbol for Israel. They had every Spiritual advantage available, and yet, they were fruitless, as exemplified by their rejection of the Messiah.

Jesus also spoke of *pruning* good vines so that they could bear more fruit (John 15:2b). In part a. of this verse; He said that those who do not bear fruit "He takes away." Later He says they are thrown in the fire. People sometimes suggest Jesus wasn't clear, but it was intentional. He used agricultural metaphors because (word removed) His audience could relate to them. It's not as cryptic today because most of us understand the reference and the point.

Fruit of the Spirit

Can we now acknowledge *fruit* can be considered the same as *profit?* John the Baptist, speaking to a group of Pharisees and Sadducees, called them "a brood of vipers": "Bear fruit in keeping with repentance." (Luke 3: 8). John MacArthur comments that while repentance itself is not a *work*, works are its inevitable fruit. Jesus says something later in Matthew 7:16-20 that closely parallels John's words. He speaks of *false teachers* and how they will be known by their fruits. Specifically, He says: "…every healthy tree bears good fruits, but the diseased tree bears bad fruit."

Christian Schwarz (2006, 80-81) points out that fruit, according to the Bible and biology, is visible and provides a way to check the quality of an organism. For a church, the main way to measure the quality is by its adherence to Biblical principles which should ultimately be reflected by its growth (multiplication). One of the principles that help to provide growth is *need-oriented evangelism.*

Paul writes in Galatians 5:22-23 that the "fruit of the Spirit is love, joy, peace, patience, kindness, goodness, faithfulness, gentleness, self-control." Can we exhibit that fruit without having something tangible to show for it? Sure, but all of these are willful acts. No exclusion is made in business transactions for committing these acts. Maybe there is a better way to say it, but I'm trying to connect business and faith.

If we have faith, we should exhibit it regardless of the venue in which we are operating. There are prohibitions against excluding these in business. For instance, we are not to go to the courts to settle matters for which the court doesn't have authority. Those are what matter in our behavior with regard to our faith and are not to be judged by the unrighteous.

Appendix questions:

- Have you ever thought of capital in the ways it was presented here?
- Do you buy the notion that it has the importance suggested?
- Do you agree capital is important to non-profits as well?
- If *fruit* is the equivalent of *profit*, can it become capital?

Appendix C

VALUE PROPOSITION

Definition: a promise of value to be delivered and acknowledged and a belief from the customer that value will be delivered and experienced. It can apply to an entire organization or parts thereof or customer accounts, or products or services.

Comments: It is part of a business strategy that is based on a premise that satisfying customers is the source of sustainable value creation. Developing a value proposition is based on a review and analysis of the benefits, costs, and value that an organization can deliver to its customers, prospective customers and other constituent groups within and outside the organization.

A value proposition is a statement which identifies clear, measurable, and demonstrable benefits customers get when buying a particular product or service.

I'm not sure we need all that, but I wanted to give some "official" information regarding value. The reason is that every buying decision has some level of value assessment involved. The significance is that we seldom do anything (word removed) we haven't seen (word removed) as worth our time and/or money to do. There are, of course, occasions when we have less of one and more of the other. The proposition dynamic will change as these factors change. In other words, the perception of the value of something will change in the mind of the customer due to factors that the supplier cannot control (more later).

Let me parenthetically say all of this about "sales" is not confined to a strictly business environment. We don't just have sales with products or services; there are also sales of the *intellectual capital* type as well. By that I mean that ideas normally have to be sold to other people as well. You could be a 4-star general in the Army sitting atop a tank and still not have anyone following you. Once when I took a strictly selling job, my mother said, "Oh, I could never do that!" She had a job in state government and had to present the department's plans to the Legislature. I told her it is some of the hardest selling that anyone does.

How Do You Assign Value?

As Robert Lupton (Lupton 2011, 2) points out: we all want to make a difference. Our actions don't always bear that out, however. Have you thought about this? What great thing would you like to do or be involved in if you had the chance? It seems, for many of us, finding something meaningful to do with our lives is an afterthought. Patrick Morley (Morley, 1999-15) describes us being pushed along by life until we get to about age 50. Then we find ourselves in the middle of a "lake" with the opportunity to finally do something we want to do. That is, of course, if you aren't in the position of being destitute. If we could back up and get involved in something meaningful early in life, perhaps we would have a path to keep us from ending up in the middle of the lake. This is not about career decisions, but it is about life decisions. Finding significant value in what you do can make a big difference.

In a business environment, you will need to evaluate the value proposition of the venture you are considering. Hopefully, you will put as much thought and research as possible into making your decision. Value equals worth. When we look at the value of something, we are determining whether it is worthy of our investment – whatever that might be. Relationships are like that as well. Unfortunately, too often we don't take the proper time and make the appropriate effort to learn all we can about our relationships.

Most of the time, relationships are not the product of a deliberate decision-making process. We make a value judgment when we first encounter other people. Depending on our experience, we will go through a very quick assessment of them. I heard this many years ago, but it seems to have changed to some extent. Too often, we don't seem to even put much effort into determining the potential value of forming a relationship with others. It is critical to our development as a person to be able relate in a way that adds value to both parties. Our most important relationship is the one we have with God through Jesus Christ. If we cannot, it will be difficult to have the proper kinds of relationships with others.

Continuing on the path of worth, much is written in Scripture about God being "worthy." Worship is both an attitude and an act. The definition of *worship* with regard to attitude is "esteem worthy." In other words, God is "worthy of esteem" and therefore has great value. The greatest value that God offers to us as humans is salvation. We, of course, are not "worthy," but we have great value to God. We should also value the commands He has given us. The amazing part about it to me is God wants the best for us. It is when we decide we know better than He does that we devalue Him and thereby ourselves. That is why it seems that value is so vitally important.

For instance, Jesus spoke of the value proposition in telling his followers to count the cost of building a tower lest people should laugh at them if they didn't have the resources to finish. (Luke 14:28) We probably tend to place the most value sometimes on our ego. Imagine Jesus telling us to prepare properly so we don't become a laughingstock. Some of us may say or at least tell ourselves we don't care what people say or think about us. In reality, though, I don't think most of us like to be laughed at. Think about how the urban gangs get so upset about being "dissed." What a notion: killing somebody because they didn't show them the proper respect. Just what does that mean anyway? Of course, it wasn't so long ago, wars were fought over the "esteem" value some felt they deserved. Heck, our schools seem to value self-esteem over achievement! I don't know; doesn't it make sense to show people how living out their purpose on earth gives one *esteem*?

OK, here's another one of those times when you may decide this is rather insensitive. At this point you should be seeing these matters somewhat from my perspective. Much of what I am about is encouraging and helping people to do for themselves. What do we teach people when they are not of enough value to learn how to make something better of themselves? I often wonder about people who don't have some aim in life. They must not know the *value* of striving to achieve something.

Factors that Lead to Relationships in Business

Relationships have value, but the extent of that value depends on a number of factors. The root word of relationships is "relation" which is normally considered a matter of family. The root of relation is "relate."

Obviously, when we relate to others, it is generally considered to be the creation of a relationship. My dad always said, "God gave you your relatives, and you choose your friends." Sometimes we have better relationships with friends than relatives, for sure. However, it has been my experience that, when the chips are down, "blood **is** thicker than water." Even after years of estrangement, God can heal broken relationships; and the best ones are the familial ones.

In sales, a distinction is made for "relationship selling." A long way into my working career I became acquainted with the term. My dad loved people, and his customers were always people he had a relationship with. For some salespeople, once a sale has been made, whatever relationship that might have existed is over. I bet you have had purchasing experiences like that. After all, in an age of self-service, we don't have much of a chance to form any relationships at all. So, when I got to the point where I was selling products or services requiring involvement in the purchasing decision, relationship selling became an important thing for me. After that, I began to realize the relationship has gone both ways; I needed to do business with people I trusted and offer more value than just a sale.

Value is very important in relationships. The relationship may become more important to keeping the customer supplied when demand stresses supply. The balancing act that relationship selling dictates is sometimes a "bone of contention." As a buyer, value to a salesperson was, if I made the decision to purchase their products, they could be sure there would never be any question about why. If I needed help from the supplier, I could get it if it was something that they had the power to do. Sometimes they would even go to their supervisor to get authorization because they felt comfortable that I would only ask for it if the benefit would accrue to all concerned.

My experience includes every place in the process of getting a product from its completely raw source to the ultimate consumer – and being a consumer myself. What you have to offer to your customer is some sort of value and generally this builds a relationship be it shallow or deep. If you have a product that has competition in the marketplace, you must have a value proposition to offer with it. If you offer a service, the same applies in that you must differentiate yourself from anyone else who offers it. These may be features, techniques, programs, delivery, customer service, pricing, or anything else that you may come up with. Some salespeople have been successful by "wining and dining" their customers, but that never worked for me. It's OK to take a buyer to lunch and pay for it if you have a long-standing relationship with them already. Hear me clearly on this: there are people who will have a relationship because the salesperson takes them on trips or whatever. Don't waste your time and money trying to undo that relationship. Buyers have gotten fired over conflict of interest, and life is too short for you to invest yourself in a mess like that.

It is also very necessary that you be careful when doing business with friends. Many people I know – including me – have been burned by trying to use a relationship as a springboard to a business venture. The reasons to avoid such arrangements are many. Some are above board and are just not the right thing to do from a business standpoint. Some are toxic in that the other person is only in it for themselves, and they will burn you at some point. Every relationship has to have value on both sides. This is sometimes considered "win-win." I've spent a lot of time studying and participating in negotiations, and you will regret participating in one if neither party is willing to make it work.

Relationships in the business world may not ever turn into sales situations, and that may be best. I've mentioned how my wife would get annoyed with her bridge club friends who bought ceiling fans from a competitor. I came to learn it was for the best. If one gets upset with the other about something to do with the business transaction, the only option that works is for both parties to be completely satisfied with the outcome. Anything else can cause the annoyance to fester and perhaps destroy the relationship. The value must be in the product or service and not be mainly personal.

Unlike what many believe, being attentive when you are seeking to make a sale doesn't necessarily lead to a relationship or a sale. However, persistence is sometimes a rare commodity; but it can be the very thing that puts you in a position to be successful. In advertising, the common belief is that it takes six "touches" for a person to decide to purchase a product or service. A *touch* is essentially a contact of awareness such as an advertisement (radio, TV, internet, Twitter, newspaper, etc.) or direct contact (telemarketing, direct sales call, referral, etc.) Personal selling is usually considered to be the most effective although it depends on the customer. Emails and pop-up internet ads are designed to get the reader to "click-through" in order to get more information. When I do that, I rarely make a phone call after looking at the pages in the chain I hook onto. When I do, it is because I have no other choice or to follow up to ensure my understanding of what has been presented is correct.

Now it is not that I don't like talking to people; it's just there have been too many times salespeople have given me the wrong information. I assume it is that they just don't know the correct answer, but they have caused me to mistrust the information they give me until I can verify it. My wife would probably say that it is because men don't like to ask for directions. My answer to her when she has said that is: I don't like being given incorrect information. Of course, some of us are problem-solvers by nature and would just rather figure it out ourselves. However, when it comes to something involving someone I have a relationship with (one that does know his/her stuff), I look to them for information, confirmation, or support. This is, of course, in cases where I am pretty sure they know what they are talking about.

Value-added Relationships

Forming relationships in a business setting can be delicate. There was a tire store and auto repair business located in a town where I once lived, and I used them frequently. Normally, when a person spends as much time and money in a business as I did, it is expected that records will be kept and reminders sent for other products or services that may be recommended in the future. I don't recall that this business did that, but they did have a changeable copy sign outside their business that said, "God loves you, and we love you." Once when my son took his car in for service, I was double charged for some work and other work was done that I didn't authorize. A relationship doesn't mean that you take advantage of it. That was the end of my patronage at that business.

I have lived in many different places and used many different auto service centers. It is not uncommon for me to receive bad service. The reputation of any business is important, but it is extremely important when the products and services affect your life or well-being. We wish all people who sell us something would care enough about how well it works for us. People just can't go around worrying about whether everything they sell is a winner with the purchaser, but we should be able to expect that somehow there is value in dealing with the person or business you choose to buy from. However, my guess is most businesses and salespeople don't give it much thought, and maybe it is because we just don't have the capacity to deal with every sale made.

It's a bit hard for me to say that I was able to have concern for every sale that I made, but I have a strong value system I can trace back to my early years of life. I'm one of those who believes we don't come into the world with a developed understanding of right and wrong. We do have the "light of conscience" given to us by our Creator, so our experiences should reinforce that. My parents raised me going to church on Sundays and at other times, but situations still arise when we don't always make the right decisions. Thankfully, I didn't get away with much. It seems good to make mistakes because we have the opportunity to grow from them. Don't think I believed that at the time; we learn over time there are consequences for our actions. Personally, I like praise better than correction/criticism. With that backdrop, I know how it feels to be caught in a lie, and I know what it feels like to be lied to. Judge Judy Scheindlin tells the litigants that come before her that you need to have a very good memory to be a liar. That's not enough for me. So, I bring the value of telling the truth when I am making a sales "pitch" (I prefer *presentation*). Some people argue honesty is not the best policy because you can be punished or miss out on opportunities if you always are honest with people. OK, so honesty may not be best, but it is the *right* policy.

Another value that can be added to the equation is: doing what is best for your customer. Please understand *customer* can describe anyone you are trying to *sell* your idea or project to. "Well, what else would you do?" you ask. Some of this is obvious – I hope. You shouldn't sell something to a person you know is dangerous for them to have. The bottom line is to be flexible and remember your value proposition is one of the most important things you have to offer.

For-profits vs. Non-profits in the Value Proposition

Part of the reason folks in churches and other non-profits have a problem with *profit* has to do with a serious double standard. When it comes to social innovation and social entrepreneurship (see Appendix J), the measures of success are determined on a different scale. Of course, the reason for this has to do with the atmosphere of benevolence hovering over any activity with *social* in the title. Let me say again – because I don't want to be mischaracterized – I am not against either of these endeavors. My number one purpose is to make sure these are "profitable," fruitful ones.

One of the best (or worst) examples of this was presented by Dan Palotta on a TED talk about his book: *Charity Case.* Palotta views the situation from a different perspective, and I'm not sure that I follow all of the logic in his presentation. However, the overriding point he makes is rock-solid, and it has to do with what I alluded to in the paragraph above. Palotta's perspective comes from being essentially driven out of business because he made too much money for his non-profit customers. He contends non-profits are not allowed to use funds for advertising and promotion, high-powered management, or basically anything allowing them to invest in their future. While this was true in his case, today, many do spend a lot on promotion, and salaries are very high in many situations.

My experience with the economic development organization is similar, yet not exactly. We got hung up over the first economic development director because two of the board members didn't want to pay what the job commanded. One of them actually gave me ammunition to lobby for hiring him when the point was made that we weren't a "prize plum" or something to that effect. After that director left, I had to change the job description so we would not be getting so many applications for a job that wasn't going to pay anywhere near what the prior jobholder got. The argument was: a "good" job in the county was with the highway department would be $10,000 per year! In other words, how could we justify paying substantially above that and not upset the people in the county? Oh, by the way, those are the same people that are on some sort of disability or public assistance.

Two churches I was a member of used the same consulting

company to do fund-raising for capital improvements. The first one was in Mississippi, and I was a member of the building committee that chose them to raise funds. What was interesting about the situation was the church had tried to do a fund-raising campaign on their own using members of the congregation. It didn't cost much, but it was a major disaster! The consulting company charged over $30,000 which was a percentage of the goal for the campaign. The actual amount was quite a bit over the goal. Would it be a surprise if I recommended the same company when I was on the building committee at the second church? Perhaps it also wouldn't be a surprise if the result was just as dramatic, would it? And, of course, it wouldn't be a surprise as well that there were a lot of people who didn't agree with the decision to pay that much for consulting.

We were fortunate because we learned before it was too late. Palotta and his successful company went out of business abruptly after raising $71 million for breast cancer research. This was due to the decision-makers becoming too concerned about the "overhead cost." The next year after Palotta's company was fired, the charity tried to do it themselves. The revenue was down 84% and the overhead was higher.

This Appendix has said a lot about value in relationships. Sincere, transparent people can more easily develop the kind of relationships that are effective and provide value. Here the saying "people don't care how much you know until they know how much your care" comes to life (or not). That's real value!

Appendix questions:

- How necessary do you feel the *value proposition* is in choosing a project to undertake?

- Value in relationships keeps them fresh and enticing. Does this mean we have to work at maintaining or growing relationships?

- It takes profit in order to maintain and expand capital. Is that as important to non-profits as for-profits?

Appendix D

Government and Business

Actually, this might more appropriately be entitled: government vs. business. You may have heard that there are three "great" lies, and one of them is: "I'm from the government, and I am here to help you." Between regulation and taxation, the government seems to be warring against business. Some countries nationalize businesses by essentially taking them over. In war times, it may make sense to be in control of certain businesses, but having taxes go to finance businesses seems to be in direct contrast with private enterprise. To be fair, it is not just the government that appears to be out to get the businessperson. The real culprit is the bureaucracy pervading corporations, as well as the government; but it also infects church hierarchy. I have said this to people who don't exactly agree with me. It's not just that people particularly like government or other bureaucracies – only the people who get something from them actually "like" them. The percentage of people in the U.S. who get benefit from the government directly or indirectly ranges from 50 to 70%. This is actually a large number of people who "like" the government for what they get from it. I know, it is an unfair characterization of people's attitudes since there are those (like me) who get from the government begrudgingly. Many, on the other hand, have spent much of their waking lives trying to get all they can.

Fortunately or Unfortunately

When I decided to go into business for myself in a big way, my first choice was to get financing directly from the bank. Unfortunately, my first partner bailed on the project due to his belief that his future was brighter where we were both working. Fortunately, after blowing through various options that would enable me to move ahead in his absence, I ended up with a contractor who told me we could use his bank. Unfortunately, his bank wanted to foreclose on him because of his projects being underwater. Fortunately, the bank recommended jettisoning my second partner and applying for a loan guaranteed by the Small Business Administration (SBA). Unfortunately, my business began to struggle under the entire debt after all went well for a while. The bank called for its guaranty from the SBA. Fortunately, the SBA was sympathetic due to my determination to make it through the difficulty. In fact, a representative from the SBA even testified in my behalf in a lawsuit I filed against the bank and my former partner. Unfortunately, I lost the suit, but I gained a greater appreciation for the SBA. It would not be fair to leave you with the notion that I became a fan; the person who worked out the arrangements was an anomaly. Most of the people I encountered in the SBA were like most government workers: totally unsympathetic to my needs. Fortunately, I got out of the business with a little cash in my pocket and everyone paid off.

Please understand it is not my intention to impugn the character of all government employees. My mother worked for the state government, and I have worked with government agencies that are more concerned with results than procedure. However, a results-orientation is not the norm with regard to most government agencies. It can be argued there are regulations, etc., these agencies must adhere to. Granted, but laws and regulations are supposed to be made to protect the citizens of this country and maintain order. In this regard, some (maybe all) are designed to restrict or "force" behavior. Milton Friedman in his essay entitled *Why Government Is the Problem* (Friedman 1993, 8) wrote that people who run our private enterprises have the same incentive as the people who are involved in government enterprises: to promote their own interest. He quoted a professor friend of his who said you can trust everybody to put their own interest above everybody else.

Assuming you are a Christian, I would also assume you take some umbrage at this characterization. I think it is fair for us to give people the benefit of the doubt, but we should also be realistic. Some would argue that, being selfish creatures, we do virtually everything out of selfish motivation. I don't want to beat that notion to death, but it is fairly easy for us to rationalize our being deserving. The point Friedman is making is the difference between a public-sector worker and a private sector worker is not that one is a good person and the other one bad. It is each one's self-interest is served by different actions in one vs. the other – a different bottom line. People who start businesses may experience success or failure in their business, and in the case of failure, they lose money. On the other hand, an enterprise started in the public sector may have the same results. However, with a different bottom line, they can argue that factors causing their failure can be overcome with funding from sources the private enterprise doesn't have access to. Certainly, there are options for private business to get additional capital, but it normally comes at a cost. I can tell you from personal experience; it is extremely hard to get funding to cover a loss.

This is, on its face, unfair competition the public sector imposes on the private one. Unfortunately, it doesn't stop there. Funding of private sector businesses by the government has gotten to the point where sometimes they are picking favorites. Elsewhere I have mentioned some recent examples, but here is one that goes back quite a few years. This has to do with the advent of manned powered flight. Ever heard of Samuel Pierpont Langley? Most people haven't – I just recently heard of him myself. It turns out he was the first great hope for manned powered flight. According to Simon Sinek, Langley had everything most people would say are necessary for success in any enterprise: adequate capital ($50,000 from the War Department), good people, and favorable market conditions. However, these didn't help Langley, and success came from two brothers – Orville and Wilbur Wright – who had none of these. What they did have was a belief they could be successful. Who do you think the government was pulling for? It is fine that people get an opportunity to start a business with so-called "built-in business." On the other hand, the reason what the government buys cost so much is that businesses have to protect themselves from the whims of people who have a different bottom line.

Another problem seems to come when the enforcement of laws and regulations involves fees and fines. One would think laws and regulation were created to keep people operating within the boundaries and "punish" them when they don't. My experience is it is more a matter of playing a game of gotcha with the citizens. One example of this, for me, came when I was applying for a loan through an SBA program that coupled banks and governmental agencies. The ostensible purpose was to lessen the burden of the risk of default. In reality (as I understand if from a former agency employee) the purpose was to exert more control over the unwitting borrowers. When I was ready to sign the papers to finalize the loan, I asked to take a couple of days to read through the contract. It was obnoxious! The entire document was small print! There were so many ways that I could be penalized for even minor deviations from the contract. I changed my mind, and I bailed on the project. It turned out to be a good thing because I wouldn't have been able to make the project pay for itself. The situation had changed in the industry since I started the process that would have torpedoed the effort.

So, as bad as this is for private enterprise, it gets worse! Public "servants" have a bias, maybe envy with regard to private businesses. Perhaps it goes beyond that. People seem to change when they have some power they haven't had (word removed) before. Sometimes it comes from being involved with a group they get some "status" from being a part of it. OK, maybe I'm being a bit judgmental, but I'm just accustomed to getting jacked around by people who seem to get some pleasure out of making it hard on their patrons. Ronald Reagan (Reagan 2004) once said, "Government's first duty is to protect the people, not run their lives."

Here's an example of what I am trying to convey in pursuing this subject. Former New York City mayor Rudolph Giuliani (Giuliani 2008) shared how he had transformed the unemployment office in the city when he was mayor. It seems the previous administration had given the workers quotas for the number of people they were obliged to sign up. Giuliani changed it so the workers were given bonuses for the number of people they placed in jobs. The results were astounding!

Of course, there is another aspect of the problem that seldom receives the light of scrutiny: the true extent of the problem of unemployment. In a report by the National Bureau of Economic Research, a dichotomy is provided that has arisen over the last four decades. From 1980 to the early 2000s there was a decline in unemployment, and there has been a decline in labor force participation since the early 2000s. Amazingly, this is due largely to the lack of desire to work among a large number of American men (10 million according to Eberstadt). The report suggests that changes in the provision of welfare and social insurance (notably disability insurance) explain about 50% of the decline in the desire to work.

Eberstadt (Eberstadt 2016, 32-35) attributes a large part of the workforce participation rate decline for men to the fact that more women are working (as does the report cited above). He believes this is due to programs targeted at women with benefits not offered to men. The construction trades, for one, have been adversely affected by the decline of men participating in the work force. When the president's Workforce initiation was launched in the spring of 2017, it was announced there were 6 million jobs available at the time. Even those who want to work have difficulty due to poor education, low job skills, or physical impairments.

Necessary "evil"?

Now, I know that we must have government, and I also know some of the comments I have made are not so positive. I spoke earlier of groups, and I think there is a positive side to being in a group. In chapter 6, I dealt with communities, and they are critical to helping areas needing revitalization. By turning groups into communities, you can begin to help people to work together in order to be successful. As long as we have groups working at cross purposes with each other it is difficult to make any real progress.

There are some programs the government offers that can be very helpful in starting businesses, creating jobs, and accomplishing real community development. Of course, then you are at the mercy of the agency offering the grant or financial assistance or whatever. It gets really frustrating going to all the trouble you must prepare applications. Then you must wait for approval or perhaps even to see if you were the winner in a competition. That's not the end of it. There are usually many hoops to jump through. This was the case with the SBA program cited above.

Again, it is not just governmental agencies that are impediments to being successful as a small business. Taxi commissions have fought Uber, the independent driver company. Recently, in St. Louis the

Auto Dealers Association sued Tesla, the innovative car manufacturer. Their complaint was Tesla was selling directly to the public rather than through dealers as the association required. Tesla closed the five dealerships in St. Louis rather than to go through costly litigation. There weren't a lot of details provided, but it sure looked like it was restraint of trade to me. I'm pretty sure the original intention was to keep GM, Ford, etc. from selling around their dealers. It shouldn't be an impediment to Tesla keeping the cost down for their customers. Unions are also notorious for running up the costs on jobs and working very inefficiently. There are "prevailing wage" contracts that require contractors to pay union scale wages when they receive these contracts. There is some benefit to the customer due to the training that union members are required to have. On the other hand, everyone ends up paying more because of the substantially higher wages the contractor is required to pay.

David Smick, in *The Great Equalizer* (Smick 2017, 1-28), points out that what he calls "Main Street Capitalism" is the only answer that works for our economy. He identifies the "Big Three" – government, big business, and the "central" banks – as the ones who control what goes on in our national economy. Basically, his reasoning is that these bureaucracies operate in ways that are in their best interest. Earlier in this Appendix I shared Milton Friedman's contention about government employees, but Smick takes this further. In a June 2016 report, Gallup lists the Confidence Ratings for American Institutions. The highest rating is for the Military at 73%, but Small Business is close behind at 68% with Police at 56%. Supporting Smick's contention of the "Big Three" are their ratings on this list: Banks at 27%, Big Business at 18%, and Congress at 6%. Small businesses and others that are not a part of these three understandably feel the deck is stacked against them.

The *Public Affairs Pulse Survey* conducted by the Princeton Survey Research Associates International in 2014 provided a somewhat different view of attitudes toward business and government. Their numbers are a little misleading when you consider the breakdown of the ethnic and political groupings. The high numbers for government are comprised of high marks given by African-American and Hispanic respondents. Conservatives and moderates both gave Big Business high marks, but liberals were still over 50%. The reasons given were for the offerings they provided in products and services, as well as supporting their stockholders; but they were rated very low on job creation. To me, it shows that many Americans are still very much dependent on the bureaucracies that are exercising so much control over their lives.

Can a bureaucracy produce solutions?

As I pointed out in the beginning, most people who work in bureaucracies aren't "out to get you" as much as they are just in it for themselves. My mother was a state government employee and got undermined by others in her office. They didn't like the effectiveness my mother was having in getting things done. In a merit-based system, employees are sometimes pitted against each other. As much as managers try to use these tools as a way to incentivize them, an atmosphere of competition can backfire and encourage backstabbing or other negative ways to better their lot. Lupton points out an example where the employees agreed to accept a reduced pay rate so that the proposed reduction in force would not be imposed. I have heard of other instances when all accepted a reduction to avoid the negative effects that would be the case if they hadn't. In these and other cases like them, many benefited when the loss to a few would have been the case otherwise. Recently, a Veteran's Administration hospital manager was reinstated after he had been fired for illegally trying to fire a whistleblower. We can thank the Civil Service System for that will piece of ridiculousness. The "real world" doesn't have any such protection for violations.

Ravi Zacharias spoke of the scenario that occurred when Vietnamese refugees were attempting to leave their country following the Communist takeover. The men were usually killed, and the women ended up in prostitution. As he related the gory details of the process, he posed the question: Could we expect government to be the answer to solving the problem? I even heard recently about how business is being affected by government involvement in getting building projects underway. Grants for various programs are uncertain much of the time based on needed funding levels not being honored.

Dr. Laurence Peter once said this about setting goals: "If you don't know where you're going, you will probably end up somewhere else." Corporations and other bureaucracies seem to have a problem with setting goals for achievement within the different departments within the organization. Obviously, there have to be corporate goals, but it's hard to get those to trickle down to the department level, much less the individual. Consequently, some information tends to get lost when bureaucracies get their hands on things. It is much easier for entrepreneurs and small businesses to effect change and to be nimble when responding to new opportunities.

All of this could be considered as my attempt to get readers to get on to the bandwagon of promoting entrepreneurial ventures. Well, it is to some extent, but mainly I want to point out a couple of things about the business world as it relates to solving problems in declining communities. I was in my dentist's office recently and picked up a Fortune magazine from 2015 (OK, I just had to point out reality). In there was a list of innovative endeavors by large corporations. Now this is very noteworthy, and I applaud such philanthropic projects that can best be done by highly-capitalized businesses. However, communities tend to get lost in these efforts.

Most mission trips that seek to do housebuilding and rehab tend to descend on rural areas or dilapidated urban neighborhoods. Most of the time, these are done by larger churches or benevolent organizations, grouped together by the common interest of doing good. Sometimes there are "boots on the ground" – people who live in the community or neighborhood and coordinate the work. Even so, these groups come in, do their work, and then go home. Not only does this not do much for community development, it also reinforces the feeling of dependency.

There was a group from a church that I once belonged to that went to work at an orphanage in Mexico. They were building a new dormitory for the children in order to replace one in great disrepair. When they were celebrating their progress near the end of the trip, they were shocked to see that the new building was on fire. They caught the culprit, an orphan boy who lived there. His reason: no one was paying any attention to him. The reactions to this event were varied. They included: outrage at such a careless act, the boy's incredible selfishness, and a great shame at the loss of labor and material that they had expended. I didn't hear anyone express shame at being focused on the building rather than the children.

Some sanity was introduced from an unlikely source: an editorial in a community newspaper (West Newsmagazine in the suburban St. Louis area published in 2011). The title of the column was *How Jobs Are Made,* and it points out the wake of the *Great Recession* did not leave the U. S. economy with a healthy job situation. The writer suggests that "desperate policymakers will attempt to employ some desperate policies" in order to solve the problem. These are the typical means of dealing with it, and they are doomed to fail. Just as Smick pointed out, mega-corporations and the government have not been successful in getting the job done. The Kauffman Foundation, the largest foundation in the world that is focused on entrepreneurship, studied the rate of job creation and job destruction over a 20-year period. They pointed out that, while existing companies are net job destroyers (at the rate of approximately 1 million jobs per year), startup companies are net job creators (at the rate of 3 million jobs per year).

The take-away from this is obviously that the way to make an impact in the job-number problem is to make the climate for entrepreneurial ventures more favorable. The following is the list of suggestions that the writer provided. They need:

1. Access to capital

2. Access to training and support (like offered at incubators)

3. Access to highly trained workers

4. Security of offering those workers reasonable benefits at reasonable rates

5. Protection of a transparent patent and copyright system

6. The efficiency of the world's greatest technologies

These are common sense requirements and are actually very affordable. The problem is they don't make headlines like announcements from government officials do. When one looks at the abysmal performance by government in making a difference, it is even more amazing we can't seem to see what a difference can be made by entrepreneurs.

One has to wonder if operating a charitable organization effectively is even possible under such circumstances. I used to have teachers and other school officials point out how much time they spend putting up with new programs that really aren't directed toward the target they should be::the students. I think the answer to the previous question is: it is difficult in the long run.

Appendix questions:

- Do you share the view that government is a "necessary evil"?
- How do you see the impact of bureaucratic organizations being an impediment to developing communities?
- What evidence have you seen that government can be detrimental to business growth?
- What solutions can there be to changing the landscape?

APPENDIX E

RISK, REWARD, AND FAILURE

One day I was sitting in my attorney's office shortly after they had redecorated the waiting area. On the wall was a print with a quote by Theodore Roosevelt:

" Far better is it to dare mighty things, to win glorious triumphs, even though checkered by failure... than to rank with those poor spirits who neither enjoy nor suffer much, because they live in a gray twilight that knows not victory nor defeat."

This was exactly what I needed to see. The occasion was for me to meet with my attorney about how to separate from my business partner. I had been told by my banker my loan request was stalled by the loan committee's concerns about my partner. It's a long story, and the risk was not over. However, I was willing to continue on my quest to get the business open even though it would be without the "benefit" of a partner. This was not the first or would it be the last time I would be faced with such challenges. My belief in the concept of the business was strong, but there are those moments in the journey to success that cause you to rethink the whole matter. When you do, you remember all that friends, family, and others have said about your sanity. Seeing this message on my attorney's wall convinced me I still had to keep going in order to get this done.

Lest I leave you with the impression everything was lovely, let me tell you the road was long and winding. In the end it didn't' turn out the way I had hoped, but I did end the saga on my own terms. When we go through situations like this, someone is going to ask if it was worth it and if you would do it all over. I mentioned earlier how Dolly Parton answered that question. She said, "I wouldn't take anything for the experience, but I wouldn't do it over again for anything." That pretty well sums it up for me. As we were reaching the end of the trial when I sued the bank and my former partner, my attorney (not the one at the beginning of this story) commented that the sad part about this whole matter is I would never do it again. I never have been really sure about what he meant, but I guess he was referring to the trial and the contentiousness that accompanied it. While true, I have certainly learned and grown stronger from the experience. I guess that means I am not one of the "cold and timid souls."

Risk

So, I shared this story to point out what George Bernard Shaw (Shaw) once wrote: "The mass of men lead lives of quiet desperation..." The reason for it may be a lack of *vision* (see more in the next section). The vast majority have to see something they want to achieve before they are willing to risk what it takes to get it. A number of the synonyms for profit have to do with reward although it isn't one of the words that usually comes up. We aren't always reasonable about what we strive for; but whether we are or not, it is amazing what we will do to get it. There are, however, people who spend a lot of their waking time trying to avoid risk.

Satchel Paige once said: "Work like you don't need the money. Love like you've never been hurt. Dance like nobody's watching." That seems like the ultimate risk to me. I never thought I had it in me to risk the way opening and owning your own business requires. Certainly, I wasn't looking to have it be in the retail arena; I had way too much exposure to that growing up. What is most interesting to me is God will lead you if you are willing to let Him. I have struggled for most of my life with having to make thousands of decisions. Some people are "control freaks" and really want to be in charge of everything. There are people who would probably say I am one of those. It's not really unreasonable to want to plan for every contingency. Of course, you can't really do it, so you do have to take risks.

It's been accurately said the greater the reward, the higher the risk – and vice versa. The first step is deciding on what you want to do. We all have dreams, but few actually act on them. Most people just settle for the hand they think they are dealt. The "luck of the draw" is how we characterize what we end up with (at the moment anyway). Keeping the metaphor going: we need to know when to hold them and when to fold them. Holding on to your dreams at least gives you the opportunity to continue your pursuit in the future. Of course, dreams can be deceptive as well as illusive. Leadership guru John Maxwell has written an excellent book on how to vet your dreams. The title is *Put Your Dreams to the Test*, and it spells out a process to make sure your dream is the one you should pursue.

In my case, my dream kept on until it fizzled or seemed to evaporate. I have often said I have never had any useless experiences. I meant learned something from every one of them. There are a lot of them that fit into the category Dolly Parton described as: not wanting to go through again. As I reflected on each experience, I could see God working in them, fashioning my character and leading me in other directions. It has also been said we learn more from failure than we do from success. Of course, it is important to recognize what success looks like. I've written about this elsewhere, and it is really a major point of this book. **How we define success has everything to do with whether or not we actually do succeed. It also has to do with our sense of well-being**.

The reason to spend time on this now is success is essentially its own reward, in many instances. When I wrote on the importance of focusing on results, I was pointing out that when we do, we are seeking real success. In doing so, we are going against the grain since the world doesn't have a Christian view of it. However, the point is our risk tolerance increases as we can see the results/reward/success that can be achieved when we step outside of our comfort zone.

Perhaps one of the greatest risks we can take is to reach out to people with the desire to make their lives better. There are some benefits that come from doing that, and failure seems to be a non-issue. I believe the reason for that is we tend to do something like swoop into a food pantry, pass out some boxes of food, and leave to go back to our lovely home and family situation. We have the feeling of doing something worthwhile, and we don't have to stick around to see the results (or lack thereof). The reward has come, to our way of thinking, in having provided a needed service. So, where's the risk, you ask?

First of all, the risk comes in not being prepared for what you encounter when you seek to serve people that are "down and out."

Some of these people will refuse some of the food, others will sell it (perhaps to buy drugs), and some will come in a Cadillac or other luxury car to pick up the food. Some actually have the temerity to wear fur coats or other expensive clothing when they come. Then, if you keep serving there, you will see these people come back time after time never feeling any "shame" at doing what they are doing. You see, the biggest risk is you have helped put these people in a state of dependency and have *taken away their dignity.* Sadly, this is what the risk really is; you haven't looked beyond the good you thought you were doing in order to see the harm that might be done.

Toxic Charity (Lupton 2011, 11-18) was the first accurate account of what happens in the lives of people who get drawn into a life of dependency. It neither starts nor ends with a food pantry. The sense of dependency comes from the enabling that comes from those who are well-intended but not well-directed. Consider the following:

- One of the ways this happens comes from the common reaction to a crisis. Tornados, floods, etc. have a wide-reaching effect on people's lives. People are killed, homes are destroyed, and jobs are lost. The appropriate response is to garner resources to take care of the immediate needs of the victims. In the case of the Joplin, MO, tornado, the outpouring was tremendous. So was the response to Ferguson, MO, even though it was not a natural disaster.
- The next step in reacting to such situations is to do everything possible to get back to the way it was before the crisis came. The natural tendency is to go beyond the previous situation in order to "over-compensate" for the loss the victims have experienced.
- The breakdown comes due to the inability of the people who are charged with trying to restore things to cope with the enormity of the situation. Contractors who tried to help local officials deal with reconstruction said they were just overwhelmed with it all. By that time, most of the volunteer help had left and government programs had begun to kick in.
- Many people left the area because they didn't have jobs or the place where they had lived was on abandoned property. It was a challenge for workers to try to find the

owners because they couldn't work on the property without permission.

- Most of the time, development is impeded by lack of interest on both sides coming as a consequence of dealing with the previous points. People get comfortable with the level reached and reviving enthusiasm is difficult at best.

Crises come in other ways than from natural disasters. For the individual, a crisis can come from losing a job, a health or medical problem, having the home repossessed, or someone going to jail. It doesn't matter what the percentages are if one of these happens to you. The effect tends to be the same. Anything that impedes a person's ability to do for themselves is potentially going to cause a downward spiral. Lupton provides this as a "progression"

- Give once and you elicit appreciation;

- Give twice and you create anticipation;

- Give three times and you create expectation;

- Give four times and it becomes entitlement;

- Give five times and you establish dependency.

After this, there are more stages: dependency becomes shame, and then comes anger at themselves for having to take charity and anger at the giver because of how they are viewed. Servers become cynical through their experiences, and it shows in their attitudes. This can be changed by involving the *clients* as they are called, and it may help put a detour on the road to despair.

You see, I have served on several mission team trips, worked on Habitat for Humanity projects, and supported and served at food pantries. What I know is most of the people who serve as I did – on a sporadic basis – usually get jaundiced about the process and just stop serving. There are those who are so invested; however, they keep hanging on, somewhat satisfied with the "results" they are getting. It is difficult to break the latter group loose from the bond they have developed. This is the reason for the extensive "essay" I presented at the beginning. There are a number of reasons why those who serve become invested to the extent they do. The one I find to be the biggest impediment to a good solution is their attitude regarding results. This book is about results, but finding a long-term solution is extremely important.

Reward

There will be outcomes of one kind or another. I've heard it put this way: One of the most disappointing things in life is to reach the top of the ladder of success only to find out that it was leaning against the wrong building! It is foolish to embark on a project of any kind without getting a picture in your mind of what you expect the outcome to be.

NCD uses a Survey to identify where a church should focus its efforts in order become a healthy church, and a healthy church is a growing church. This step provides the "What." NCD identifies six Growth Forces (Schwarz 2006, 70-81) that should be at work during the process within a church wanting to grow. This is the "How" step. Tapping into the Growth Force(s) that are appropriate enables the Acts 2:47 concept of God providing the increase. It is a very organic process capitalizing on the value the church itself brings to the table.

While NCD is for "church" improvement, the principles have a lot of application in any setting. Of course, church people are generally a part of the mission activities, so there is certainly an overlap. In the case of Growth Forces, the one most applicable to *reward* is *fruitfulness*. The importance of this process is pointed out by Peter Drucker (Drucker) who wrote: "There is nothing so useless as doing efficiently that which should not be done at all." This goes to underscore the importance given to this force elsewhere in the book.

Absent a crystal ball, there is no way to know exactly what the outcome of a project will be. However, as Drucker points out, some projects just shouldn't be undertaken. Having a heart for some concept is not enough although many people charge out with their high-minded ideals in hand. One of the best approaches I have encountered suggests you begin with the end in mind. Vision is one of the most important components of any endeavor, but it is sometimes in short supply as I mentioned earlier. If you can envision the end result of a project that you are considering, you have made an important step toward a successful outcome.

A lot of discussion was presented in Chapter 2 when the necessity of a plan was covered. It guarantees all of what has been written and more due to its supreme importance. In addition, planning to have a profit or gain must include what it will look like. It may be the odds will be insurmountable as you work through your planning, but it is better to know in the beginning than get to the point where you have failed to accomplish much of anything.

Failure

It seems that all of us have some aversion to risk. That's not a bad thing – to a point. I mentioned earlier that risk generally increases with the value of the reward. Most of the time, this is true with regard to the price of failure as well. While it is true one needs to define what success looks like, it is also important to consider what failure is. Jim Rohn said, "It's too bad failures don't give seminars. Wouldn't that be valuable? If you meet a guy who has messed up his life for forty years, you've just got to say, 'John, if I bring my journal and promise to take good notes, would you spend a day with me?'" I haven't been a failure for that much time, but I certainly want to help people avoid many of the mistakes that are out there.

The reason for this is for you to weigh the cost of failing against the value of success (see Appendix C). All of us are probably risk-averse when it comes to physical pain or danger, but emotional pain is sometimes greater with regard to making decisions. Much of what goes through our minds when considering the likelihood of failure is the attitudes of others. Eugene Peterson in *The Message* tells of the conversation Jesus had with His disciples in Luke 14:28-30.

"Is there anyone here who, planning to build a new house, doesn't first sit down and figure the cost so you'll know if you can complete it? If you only get the foundation laid and then run out of money, you're going to look pretty foolish. Everyone passing by will poke fun at you: 'He started something he couldn't finish.'"

We can all relate to that, and it's probably why Jesus used it as an example. He goes on to clarify the point He is making whatever we do, we should be "all in." This story is usually considered in the discussion about the cost of discipleship. A lot of the time, failure is due to not putting all we have behind the effort to succeed. Planning is pretty important in determining (to the best of your ability) the resources you will need to take on the challenge. Getting back to the story, Jesus is talking about the cost. Earlier in verse 17, He told those walking along with Him they would have to leave everything behind to follow Him. He also said they had to "take up their cross" and follow behind Him. The key word in this is "follow." His analogy takes a little for us to process, but He is consistent in saying there is significant cost to be His disciple. Some of that cost may come in being outside of your comfort zone. The risk seems pretty clear from that perspective. Following Jesus requires faith in Him and a willingness to risk everything by leaving and carrying a cross not of your choosing.

So, how do we fail in our role as a disciple? Well, we already covered one big way, but there are others. Some of these are directly related to the task we are engaged in, but another big one is: giving up before you have done all you are called to do. In chapter 1, I related a story about perseverance. When you think about it, by following Jesus we end up on an adventure that won't be fully revealed until long after it is over. Our faith is crucial in making sure we "stay the course." We won't always succeed, but we must learn from our mistakes.

Speaking of mistakes, here is an acrostic to describe how we can understand what they are:

(M)essages that give us feedback about life.

(I)nterruptions that should come to us to reflect and think.

(S)ignposts that direct us to the right path.

(T)ests that push us toward greater maturity.

(A)wakenings that keep us in the game mentally.

(K)eys that we can use to unlock the next door or opportunity.

(E)xplorations that let us journey where we have never been before.

(S)tatements about our development and progress.

Every statement in the above list is a positive one. That is quite appropriate because the way we think about mistakes is normally negative. This section addresses failure, and sometimes we equate mistakes with failure. If we learn from our mistakes – which is what we must do – we can avoid failure in many cases. Even if we end up in failure, much can be gained from that experience as well.

Leadership guru, John Maxwell, in his book *Failing Forward* (Maxwell 2000, 27-32) shared seven abilities needed in order to "fail forward". Achievers:

1. Reject rejection – you are what you think.

2. See failure as temporary.

3. See failure as isolated incidents.

4. Keep expectations realistic.

5. Focus on strengths.

6. Vary approaches to achievement.

7. Bounce back – failure does not make you a failure.

Perhaps you have held yourself back or find yourself getting down because of your attitude toward failure. It can be helpful to spend some time learning more about the importance of thinking positively about those speed bumps or potholes you encounter. Maxwell's book is a great source, but there are some other approaches as well. The Natural Church Development (NCD) program includes a section on "Empowering Leadership", and a segment of it has to do with how we deal with failure. Much of the program deals with what is called "the minimum factor", the weakest link in the chain. However, it is pointed out that leadership must deal with its strengths and weaknesses at the appropriate times. While businesses tend to focus on minimizing mistakes, churches and other nonprofits more likely tend to overlook them.

John Maxwell (Maxwell 2000, 12) says "One of the greatest problems people have with failure is that they are too quick judge isolated situations in their lives and label them as failures. Instead, they need to keep the bigger picture in mind." He firmly believes that failure is an opportunity to learn, but that's not all. Reinforcing bad behavior only works to make it normative.

Appendix questions:

- There is *risk* in any activity. How do you view the possibility of risk before undertaking an activity?

- This section showed that *failure* can be positive. How can that be?

- How important is it that mistakes be evaluated to avoid being ignored?

APPENDIX F

WORLDVIEW

There seem to be a lot of people who don't know what "worldview" is. One simple definition is: the way someone looks at the world. Meriam Webster's definition is a comprehensive conception or apprehension of the world especially from a specific standpoint. More are aware of the concept of "paradigm." In science and philosophy, a paradigm is a distinct set of concepts or thought patterns, including theories, research methods, postulates, and standards for what constitutes legitimate contributions to a field. Most of the time *paradigm* is used to describe the "box" that we form around our thinking. This has been created by several factors: learning, experience, observation, and relationships. OK, relationships are formed in large part by the other two, but what is shared by them is special in that we give more credence to such things in that context. I may be cutting this a little fine, but there are probably other subtle ways that our paradigm is created. I don't recall much being said about how *worldview* is created, but my guess is that *paradigm* must have a lot to do with the development of a worldview. After all, we don't consider much beyond the boundaries of our paradigm, so our *world* tends to end at them.

Paradigm shifts occur when new information/knowledge is introduced into the existing paradigm. Now, it's not in my DNA to jump on the "next new thing", but many people just resist this introduction. In another area, I provided the "theory of human behavior." If we have stopped learning, new information is not going to affect our paradigm. We have to work with what we have, so we must find ways to make this introduction in a way that people will see the benefit.

Paradigms and worldviews aren't necessarily based on truth. G.K. Chesterton said that "Truth is stranger than fiction because we made fiction to suit ourselves." I have heard some people say that it is just too hard to have to deal with reality (truth). Pontius Pilate asked Jesus, "What is truth?" Former Arkansas governor and presidential candidate, Mike Huckabee, has said, "You are free to have your own opinion but not your own facts." However, even if the facts are correct, what they comprise may not be the truth. Let me explain (if I can). The facts that are presented in a certain situation may not be the ones that reveal the truth. There are a lot of facts about cars, but they have nothing to do with something that is going on with the car. Not to get too technical, but here's an example: the car may not be running properly, but facts about the finish probably don't have anything to do with it. Here's one that relates directly to a situation that I have been involved in. The story of the dam breach that I mentioned elsewhere was blamed for several businesses closing. There were some that reached the "tipping point" for sure, but most of the businesses weren't benefiting from the tourism traffic anyway. So, it didn't matter that the fact of the breach was true. What was not true was that most of the businesses that went out were a direct result of the breach.

Facts Are Important – When They Fit

Here's the point: having your facts right and fitting the situation (or result) is critical to be able to solve the problem you are dealing with. Let's take this a step farther. When I moved to the area where the breach occurred, I was told that the problem was there weren't any jobs. Naturally, the reason was that the businesses went under because of the breach. It was my objective to try to help them rejuvenate the economy. Businesses that hire people are an important way to create the kind of economic activity that can turn a sluggish economy around. See, all of that is true, but the fact is that the reason that most of the businesses went out had nothing to do with the breach. In one case, a chain retailer and a fast-food restaurant went out because of corporate problems. Most of the businesses went out because of poor management or the owner getting old or sick and deciding to give it up. Businesses that have moved into the area haven't been able to get the kind of workers that they require to operate successfully.

So, what does this mean in the way of trying to determine what *Real* Profit is? Here are some components of a Worldview from Ravi Zacharias in *Why Jesus?*

1. It must have a strong basis in fact – is it truth?

2. Have a high degree of coherence or internal consistency.

3. Must have a reasonable & logical explanation for the various undeniable realities around us.

4. Avoid the extremes of too complex or too simplistic.

5. Not explained by one line of evidence.

6. Explain contrary world views without compromising its own essential beliefs.

7. Cannot argue just on the basis of private experience but must have an objective standard.

8. Must justifiably explain the essential nature of good and evil since this differentiates humanity from others.

I heard a report that said that only 4% of millennials have a Christian worldview. The story that they have been told, in many cases, is that there is no God or eternal life. They have been told that it is OK to drink alcohol, use drugs, smoke cigarettes or whatever, have sex outside the sanctity of marriage, and that divorce is a good reason for couples to live together without marriage. So, why would they have faith in a religion that can't stand up to a barrage of debate about how we got here in the first place? Add to that the criticism that comes from Hollywood and the media – not to mention friends, family members, and acquaintances – when our churches don't seem to do much to confront the objections to our faith. All of the things I have cited cry out for support that leads to the points that Zacharias lists.

In Ephesians 4:15 we are instructed: "Instead, speaking the truth in love, we will grow to become in every respect the mature body of him who is the head, that is, Christ." Charles Colson said, "Christianity is an explanation of all truth. Christianity is under-standing all of life. It is the glue that holds civilization together…We are to engage our culture in winsome and loving ways." This seems to me like a *worldview* that fits who we are to be as Christians: mature in our faith and knowledge of Christ.

Who Cares?

For the most part, we just don't want to think about such things as how we acquired our faith or what it really means to be a Christian. With this being the case, it is no surprise that people are not overly concerned about things eternal. We still have some religions/denominations that have the faithful going from door to door handing out tracts and/or spending large quantities of time attempting to proselytize those who will listen. Many people just don't want any part of that.

I had experienced people who would come up to me in a church hallway and start quoting Scripture to me. Then there were those who would monopolize the conversations in a Sunday School class trying to impress others with their knowledge (some people might say that I have become that way – Oh, my!).

Mission trips were considered to be evangelistic in some ways, but most of them didn't really do much to try to disciple people. More about that later, but suffice it to say, none of these approaches did anything to get me interested. However, when I was introduced to the Natural Church Development Quality Characteristic of *need-oriented evangelism*, I found a realistic approach.

It doesn't make sense to try to cram all that is involved in this important characteristic into a short consideration. However, the point is that, while evangelism is better left to those who have the gift, we are all called to be evangelistic when we have been given the opportunity to do so. We can be more pro-active in this endeavor by participating in activities that reach people where they are. In other words, showing the love of Christ by helping people in their time of need can do more to attract people to Christ than most traditional methods. By doing so, there can be the chance of sharing how you came to faith or what drives you to be a Christian. In 1 Peter 3:15, we are told to be ready to share our faith story. This means working through the above list and understanding what your faith means to you in a way that is compelling.

Mentoring others can also be a very effective way to share your faith as well. Business ethics is sometimes considered to be an oxymoron. Many people think that business is a *zero-sum game*. This means that somebody wins, and somebody loses. This seldom provides satisfying results. Trying to "bury" your competition can mean that you diminish yourself. Trying to encourage others to do the same is certainly a bad plan as well. I still believe that a "rising tide lifts all boats." This doesn't mean that we should be naïve, and the Bible doesn't suggest that we should be. Sharing yourself and your faith is what we are called to do. In the Great Commission in Matthew 28:19-20, Jesus told us to "Go!" That is: "Go therefore and make disciples of all nations, baptizing them in the name of the Father and of the Son and of the Holy Spirit, teaching them to observe all that I have commanded you...."

Expand Your Paradigm

Basically, the point is that our world has to extend beyond our paradigm. More than ever before, the world is interconnected. Terrorism has come to our shores, and how we deal with that has bearing on all of our lives – even if we don't think so. Foreign hackers take control of computer systems and demand a ransom to release them. That strikes close to home, but travel has become a major pain at best. We are involved in several conflicts around the world in the form of direct and indirect military force. Refugees and others seeking to better their lives have been pouring over our borders with many of them outside the realm of the authorities. Not only are some of these being used by drug smugglers and others, but now we are experiencing dangerous gangs wreaking havoc in parts of the country. Add to this the decline of the moral fabric of our culture, and you can perhaps understand how important it is for us to do what we can to come to an understanding of who we are as a people of God.

The notion of *worldview* is important in having true *community*. The aspects of each are very similar in that without a great deal of commonality in how the members view the world around them, true community will be hard to achieve. In a mobile world, residents of a community need to become *members*. The factors that militate against forming a community must be addressed. The fact they are so infrequently done doesn't mean we can avoid doing so without paying a high price. Small groups tend to be able to pull this off sometimes, but church groups desperately need to work through the process. It can be more easily done there if some important steps are taken. A

Spiritual Gifts Assessment for Christian groups can help identify where individuals can best use what has been entrusted to them. There are some additional programs to help form a community dealt with in Chapter 6.

Appendix questions:

- Were you aware of the concept of *worldview* prior to reading about it here?

- Do you agree that it is very important that it be considered in seeking to create community?

- Does the list of components of a worldview make sense in light of attempting to grow together in a community setting?

-

Appendix G

TRIBALISM

There are still places in the world where cultures are divided into tribes much like they have been from almost the beginning of time. Even animals tend to gather in tribe-like packs. We are a gregarious people, for the most part; but many of us aren't comfortable in crowds. Loneliness is a big problem today, and it is amazing considering how many people there are on earth. Communication is amazing, and yet we don't seem to know very much. That is most likely due to what Ronald Reagan (Reagan 2004) was conveying when he said: "...it is not that they are ignorant; it is just that they know so much that is not true." All of this tends to create a situation like what we have currently: people banding together in groups to get what they want or to preserve their way of life.

Tribes tend to have something that naturally connects them. They may be related to each other, but this only goes so far since incest leads to its own set of problems. When the Israelites were taken into exile by their enemies, God warned them about intermarriage with their captors. Like most warnings, there were lots of them who didn't heed it. There are religions that seek to prohibit marriage outside of their faith. If you are Protestant, you share that distinction with over 300 denominations. Each denomination has something that differentiates it from the others. Some are more restrictive than others about marrying a person from another denomination. Islam and Judaism are generally more restrictive in that regard, but much of that has to do with how strongly a person adheres to those and other restrictions.

What we seem to have more of today is "clannish" groups. They are quite "tribal" in nature in that they seem to have the same characteristics regarding how they become a group (however it is comprised). The ones that become more of a concern are generally known as *cults*. What makes this so is that cults normally have rules and conditions that are outside of the mainstream, and they require "allegiance" to their basic tenets. Most of these groups do not seem to want to be called cults. I would expect it is because some of what they do is illegal.

It has always been puzzling to me as to why some of the groups form in the first place. Further, I have been equally amazed as to how their leaders were chosen. In Biblical times, the choice came from family hierarchical processes leading to a succession within the family. Middle to far eastern cultures and American Indians seem to have used some sort of contests involving physical skills centered on fighting. Elections were first used by Greeks and Romans around the time of Christ's time on earth. Still, the "divine right of kings" was and still is in force. However (comma removed) it was communicated, these leaders called upon the blessing of God or some other sort of deity to support their notion that they were to lead their people. Elections led to political parties who held differing opinions on matters affecting their constituencies. Some tribes voted on important matters, but even the dictators of today are pretty much autocrats.

Malcolm Gladwell, author of *The Tipping Point*, described many brains, by exclusion, that don't have much capacity for connecting with a large portion of the population. Neurologists suggest that this is why tribalism is an inescapable fact of society. Once these brains have reached their capacity to make connections with others, they must devise some sort of scheme to keep track of them.

Dr. John MacArthur in *Joy Rules* (MacArthur 2018) points out that the Greek word for love in Philippians 1:9 is *agape*. Here Paul writes: "It is my prayer that your love may abound more and more, with knowledge and all discernment" (ESV). Here's how he sees this: "It is decisive love – the word *agapē* means the love of the will, or the love of choice, not emotion. It is dynamic love, it abounds more and more, increasing and overflowing. It is deep love, in that it is rooted in deep spiritual knowledge and understanding. And it is discerning love, in that it has insight into all the situations of life and knows how it should be applied." So, he describes a scenario where a group starts out with a fellowship, they believe to be *agape*. Later they become drawn into *nepotism* (only family) or *cronyism* (only friends). Discerning love is no longer a part of it. They become inwardly focused to the exclusion of outsiders.

We found out in Afghanistan that dealing with all the tribes made for difficulty in coming to a collective moral. So, what exists is a delicate balance being maintained by the government of the country. When some of the tribes moved away from that and supported the Taliban, a group of tribes formed the Northern Alliance. This had the support of the U.S. and other nations who opposed the Taliban. Once we invaded the country and sought to restore a democratic government, we found just how difficult it is to try to get all these tribes on the same page.

It is my feeling that dealing with large urban areas is much the same as a country like Afghanistan. There are groupings that might approximate the nature of tribes, and some of the most significant ones are gangs of mainly ethnic young people. During the "Black Lives Matter" period, the U.S. has seen protests that exhibit the control these groups can exert on an otherwise peaceful populace. It's hard to know what makes some gangs form and become so violent. The "Crips" and the "Bloods" are two that seem to always be in contention with each other in cities. Their roots date back to the years after WWII when racial segregation and poverty led the young black men to form into groups. While there were territorial considerations, there were financial issues as well.

Organized crime fits the model of tribes in many ways. Mostly, they were referred to as "families." They were essentially comprised of the same ethnic groups although that changed in years following the Prohibition era structures. Most of their focus was on engaging in activities which brought them wealth by illicit means. They were quite violent and "gang wars" broke out on a fairly frequent basis. It has always amazed me to hear of the pervasiveness of their involvement in various industries. A former "Mafia don" said that the "mob" infiltrated the unions to worm their way into the industries that the unions represented.

Facing misery (perceived or real)) creates a common bond for people to be drawn to. Organizers or leaders who can communicate effectively can use this to build their ranks. Arrogance sometimes comes from success and causes people to be inattentive to constituents.

What I am referring to is how these "tribal" groups reach the point of being successful enough that they aren't necessarily concerned about recruiting more members.

The Nazis in World War II showed how powerful propaganda can be. I have to feel it has been this way throughout history. People tend to ignore the sources they feel are not telling them the straight story. What happens in the U.S. today is that "trusted" news sources are aligned politically, and far too much opinion is included in what is purported to be news. News people mostly want to report something controversial, so they are quick to jump on a story that would further inflame the passions of the competitors. Some people like good news, but mostly people seem to want something tantalizing. Otherwise, our news sources wouldn't be full of that stuff. The point is all of this is pandering to some group. We tend to become synthesized to what is directed toward us. It is so insidious and so pervasive that we hardly know it is going on. Now, I know this is not universally true, but let's say you have an affinity for an athletic team. The team could be from a school you went to or whatever. I mean, they call people who support such teams' "fans" (short for "fanatics"). It's has amazed me – even in myself - that people can get so passionate about things that really don't matter. The only thing I can figure out is being a part of a group enables us to live vicariously through the group. But it's why we follow celebrities, isn't it? Someone once said we are smart as individuals but ignorant as a crowd.

Think about how different it would be if you were part of a group that actually did something meaningful. Of course, I mean something more than sitting around and commiserating with each other or complaining about the price of eggs (oh, we don't do that anymore, do we?) or whatever. What a difference it could make to be a part of something bigger than yourself; something that makes a difference. Focusing on results is what makes the difference and being a part of a group with that mindset is how you can have it.

Who is calling the shots for you? Are you being led by a "tribal leader," someone who has risen to the top of the heap by rather draconian methods? Have you risen by hard work and then been elected/chosen to be the leader? What kind of group are you in? Do you just sort of go along with the crowd? What drives you to do what you do?

The answers to these questions will have a tremendous bearing on how successful you can be at creating a healthy community that has the potential to be successful.

Appendix questions:

- *Tribalism* is everywhere. Where have you seen the effects of it?
- Do you see yourself as belonging to a group that exhibits tribalistic attributes?
- What do you think is the likelihood these types of groups can do positive things?

Appendix H

COMMUNICATION

This topic could be a part of the Cs in S.U.C.C.E.S.S. It certainly has to do with the ability to achieve *community*. We have thousands of thoughts every day. Most of them don't get past the "walls" of your cranium, and that is probably a good thing. There was a movie starring Jim Carrey entitled *Liar, Liar* (Universal Pictures, 1997) where Carrey could only tell the truth about what he was thinking. As bad is this was for him, it is not nearly as bad as it would be if every thought were expressed out loud. People would tend to ignore most of what was being said because it would take all the oxygen out of the room. My mother had Alzheimer's disease, and she got to where she would tell stories she could remember, over and over again. It didn't do any good to remind her that she had just told a story she was now repeating for the umpteenth time. My understanding of the nature of this condition kept me from getting agitated by her doing this, but it made me realize just how annoying it would be to hear whatever came into a person's consciousness without any filtering.

This process of *filtering* is something that we develop over time. At some point early in life we learn that no one wants to hear everything that comes to mind. It's probably due to being told by one or more people we are talking too much. Mothers may put up with a child's blathering because she loves the child and doesn't want to discourage them from expressing themselves. At some point, even a mother must let the child know that people don't want to hear all that they have to say. For one thing, most people don't learn anything by hearing themselves talking. They are just so ego-centric they want to command their audience's attention. Of course, the possibility exists where some people just feel they are the expert to be heard over other disparate opinions. Admittedly, I must be very careful, so I don't shuck the cloak of humility myself.

Once several years ago I led a Sunday School discussion regarding the fact that, in the age of mass communication, we don't seem to be able to communicate very well these days. We have 24/7/365 "journalism" on TV and on the internet, yet these are so opinionated, the truth seems illusive. Newspapers are rapidly becoming passé. Citizen journalism is taking over via a decentralized, mobile delivery technology. Everybody is an opinion expert. I refuse to use Twitter because it just seems to be more information than I want to know.

Let's take this to its next logical conclusion: If your opinion is as good as mine or anyone else's, how do we discriminate between them? Something has to give. Depending on the nature of the discussion, there must be a judge. *Public opinion* will rule in many cases. That's a pretty large audience, so most of us don't get the chance to influence it. When you feel your opinion has as much value as anyone else's, you may not care about others. That doesn't usually suffice though. Social media is rife with so many differing opinions. Believe me, I have had exchanges with people who have posted something contrary to the truth about a matter. The truth doesn't matter to many of these people if it is contrary to what they want to believe.

You can add to this what psychologists refer to as *learned helplessness* (Smick 2017, 116) This is when bad news has been so relentless for so long that people eventually become numb to it. They assume that nothing can be done to regain control over their fate that leads to subtle, benign optimism. There is something in the human psyche that forms a line of optimistic defense in the face of heart-stopping threats.

What we do listen to gives us the feeling we are at the mercy of forces that keep us from getting ahead. Everywhere we turn we find roadblocks preventing us from achieving what we want to become. Consequently, we basically give up on "getting ahead" to settle for what we are allowed to have.

To move beyond our current state of being we must be able to communicate a message that resonates with those we seek to convince. Most people can be won over if the decision is easy. We use a lot of non-verbal communication. Maya Angelou (Angelou) said that: "At the end of the day people won't remember what you said or did, they will remember how you made them feel." I had a personal example of that when I gave a testimonial at church. Another member, who had by then given her own testimonial, said she was encouraged by mine. Before I could get to feeling too much pride over being so eloquent, she went on to say she didn't remember what I had said; she just felt like she could do it after hearing my testimonial. Humility returned in a big way.

I would like to hope there was something about my experience that prompted her to feel the way she did. My guess is that it was the personal story I shared in my testimonial. One of the best ways we can win people over is to be open and honest. Opening up about things that are keeping you from healing can be great therapy. It is also a gateway to connecting with people in a meaningful way. A lot of what the Walk to Emmaus program (see Chapter 1) is about is Christians sharing with each other to help grow beyond the difficulties that we face in life. I have given several talks, and I used the same story I did in my testimonial for most of them. Once when I chose a different one, I got more positive comments than I did after all the times I gave the other one. The one I gave the most was a personal one – one that we can relate to on that level. The other one was about reaching out to a needy person, and it showed I could move out of my comfort level to help someone when it wouldn't have any direct benefit to me. Guess which comments I cherish the most.

Non-verbal Signals

A University of California study found that 93% of communication is non-verbal. This relates mainly to tone of voice or body language.

Body Language

On an episode of *The Dog Whisperer*, Cesar Millan (Millan 2017) was working with a client who had a dog that was afraid of horses. There was a wonderful story a "horse whisperer" shared about his son who was partially paralyzed. The son had worked with a horse until he could compete with full-functioning adult riders. Cesar commented that dogs and horses didn't care about disabilities or other things that humans care about. They were discussing the fact that *body language* is the universal means of communication.

It has fascinated and scared me that our most effective means of communication is something we can't seem to control – and we may not be aware we are doing it. It is so subtle it passes our notice until we are paying attention to someone who is sending off signals that catch our notice. I have learned that being able to make good presentations requires us to pay attention to it. At first, I got annoyed by the signals I picked up from people in the audience when I was presenting. Part of my self-training in being a better presenter was to remember what I heard John Cotter, the founder of the True Value Hardware organization once said: "The customer may not always be right, but (he/she) is always the customer." If you are going to successfully convince the prospect to become a customer, you need to determine if they really need what you are selling. By the way, everyone has "customers" who are buying what you are selling, or not! So, you should think about what I am sharing in the light of your situation.

Body language is the most universally used mode of communicating without words as stated above. What this consists of is a variety of actions: crossing arms, yawning, not making eye contact, reading something while you are speaking (especially smart phones, tablets, etc.), twisting in their seat and some extreme ones like making noise and/or walking out on you. I actually did have a prospect go to sleep while I was speaking, and the only other person in the room was another company representative. These are extreme, but they are very real.

People may frown or shake their head when you make a statement, but these can be opportunities to address their concern. Worst case, it may save you a lot of time you would have spent trying to win them over when it just wasn't going to happen anyway. Doing research will let you know whether there is even any reason to be talking with this person at all. It will also give you a sense of how successful you might be when you do finally meet them face-to-face.

The best way to avoid wasting a lot of time is to do research and ask questions about the prospect (the one that you are trying to in over) so that you can better understand their needs. The best way to do that is to ask leading questions to get the prospect to think about their needs regarding what you have to offer. Your body language as you are asking questions says a lot about what your intentions are. Most people aren't good at being phony enough to hide their true feelings about you. If you are just looking to put another "notch in your belt" by making the sale or whatever, you will give off signals you probably aren't even aware of. It has become a lot easier for me to be sincere in such situations because I am. I've tried to sell something I wasn't "sold on" myself or didn't know enough about the product/service to be able to make a judgment about the applicability to my prospect. Now I have learned to avoid being "found out" by preparing.

Of course, that doesn't mean you get the sale – just because you ask questions. People have their own opinions, and they may not be the same as yours. I learned as a sales rep for consulting contracts that it is easy to see the source of the problem the prospective client was having in many cases. If you ask enough good questions, it will probably become very clear to you. HOWEVER, it is quite possible that the prospect doesn't see it the way you do. As a consultant, you don't want to reveal the prescription for the problem. You want to tell the prospect that you know what the cure is and then get them to hire you to do the work. There's not anything mercenary about doing that; people will try to do it themselves and not do it very well. Even people that used the company I worked for chose them to do subsequent engagements. They knew it would be difficult for them to do it themselves.

So, what this has to do with communication and body language is you must be very sensitive to the signals the prospect is giving off. If you get too excited about determining the efficacy of your solution, you may miss how the prospect is processing this information. Decision-making is generally a process in cases like this. Objections may be valid when the prospect is trying to make a good decision. Believe me, it is agonizing for some people to make decisions, in many cases. When you are talking about several thousand dollars, it really is important to make the right choice. If you can learn to read peoples' non-verbal signals, you can pick up on a lot of what they are thinking. This is not something you learn quickly; it starts with getting to know yourself first.

Tone of Voice

Basically, the main way we convey emotion is by using *tone* in our speech. It is considered *non-verbal* because it is not the words being used as much as it is the emotional component. One of the real problems in using email and social media to express our thoughts is that it is not possible to include *tone*. This is a vital part of being able to communicate effectively. This is why I like to be face-to-face when having a meaningful conversation. Tone and body language coupled with words makes the impact complete.

You may remember that when email became so pervasive some people would have all caps in the text. This was mainly due to people being used to older computers that required caps. Emailers were cautioned to use upper and lower case so the tone would not be a shout – the way all caps were interpreted.

Emojis are sometimes used. You know, the "happy face" symbols that now have all sorts of faces besides happy ones. I never can find the one I think would represent my feelings, so I must substitute something.

Words basically have to suffice in these media. I'm a great proponent of using effective words, but without non-verbal communication, the entire meaning is not present. If you add the fact that people tend to not read all of email text, you have a lot that is missed.

Emotional Intelligence

Psychology Today (March 22, 2017) defines emotional intelligence as "the ability to identify and manage your own emotions and the emotions of others." Translating it into more recognizable language: this is the ability to recognize your own emotions and keep them under control while being able to understand the emotions of others and how they affect their work.

The benefits of having an organization that understands and practices *emotional intelligence* (EQ for emotional quotient as opposed to IQ) include:

1. Better communication – we have already considered the value

of body language and tone, and emotion is the driving force behind that. They both have a tremendous bearing on how we communicate with one another.

2. Even temperament – being able to remain calm is of great benefit in being able to think clearly rather than reacting before thinking the matter through.

3. Co-worker rapport – there's no doubt that the ability to quickly relate to others in a positive manner is of great benefit when becoming a part of a team.

4. Understanding client needs – clients don't always know what they want. Being able to get them to open up about their operation can sometimes give insight into what is going on with them. As stated above, asking good questions can be very beneficial, and the ability to do that comes from achieving a high EQ.

5. Proactivity and foresight – Much of life is about timing. In reality it is not our timing that counts; it is God's. Being able to be proactive means we can avoid being victims of circumstances. We need to be emotionally intelligent so we can be better at predicting behaviors and understanding why people act as they do. By doing so, assessments can be made based on strengths and weaknesses.

Communicating for Success

My first real challenge was in the U.S. Air Force as Material Facilities Officer. I had worked in other positions, but they were only where I had to keep my boss happy. In Mat Fac, as it was known, I was on par with other department heads. Mat Fac handled all the products that came into the base. Some were consumable items that were replaced in stock when they were requisitioned by a "customer." However, a large and very different product group was the equipment department. It was run by a civilian, and that gave him a lot of power. He had been there about 20 years, as I recall; and he knew where all the bodies were buried. He also knew how to make life miserable for people like me who were new to the system.

It was my choice to go visit with him and ask him how I could make his job easier (not literally). He could not have been better to work with. We hit it off from the beginning. There were many times I got into difficult situations, and he came through every time to help me get through them. Not only that, but he would also give me a "heads up" when there was something going on that I needed to be aware of. I have tried to do it in any similar situations I have encountered since then. They didn't all work out as well, but it has turned out to be a standard operating procedure (SOP) for me.

I've heard it said, all things being equal, people prefer to do business with folks that they like. Things not being equal, they prefer to do business with people they like. I don't know about other people, but I prefer to do business with folks I am comfortable with. I was a buyer for a wholesale hardware distributor for a few years, and I did purchasing for two of my own businesses after that. My job depended on doing the best I could do for my boss whether it was me or someone else. In some cases that meant I had to do business with people I wasn't friends with. Some of them were companies that didn't even have sales reps that called on me. There were all sorts of reasons why I chose them. To be fair, I didn't choose all of them; some were chosen for me by my boss or by associations with the company.

Generally, when a decision is made to buy a product or service from a company or individual, the determination has been made that the provider is quality one. This is not always the case, however, sometimes price or some other consideration has driven the choice. When it is based on a relationship, it is a hard bond to break, in many cases. That, of course, can be good or bad. It's good if you are the favored one. I have had some of those, and they are worth their weight in gold. A relationship should be based on trust and integrity. I have found that a fair arrangement that has created such a relationship should be allowed to remain. In such a case, I have found it a good practice to maintain your principles. Changes occur, and you may have a chance to form your own relationship when they do.

Building Relationships with Good Communication

It seems to me there isn't much of a relationship without good communication. One definition of *relationship* considers the *interpersonal* one: a strong, deep, or close association or acquaintance between two or more people. Many times, people who are connected to others through birth or marriage as *relations*. Another dimension is considering the root *relation* as being the proximity or closeness to something. In most contexts, relationships are a condition of closeness.

Rev. Michael E. Williams advocates storytelling as the best medium to reach people in a meaningful way. He believes that "stories create a network of relationships":

1. A relationship is created between the teller and those who hear the story. Context and presentation have a lot to do with it.

2. A story creates a relationship between the two above and the characters in the story itself. When you can relate to one or more of them, you can possibly carry that on throughout your life.

3. Through stories we can relate our outer world to our inner world that can be known as "imagination", "spirit", or "faith." This has to be grounded, but it offers a journey to what can be.

4. Stories "hold the mystery and meaning together, and therefore they hold the power to put us in touch with the divine." They can help us to move past the notions we have about reality to see that there is *more*.

In a world where we get so much of our information via the wired world, taking time to delve into stories can open possibilities and find a way to better communicate with the world around us. My dad was a storyteller. It got a bit tedious for me and others in that he would tell them over and over again. As I grew into adulthood, I came to understand the value of this mode of communication. I see a lot of Dad in how I communicate with others (Hello! I did write this book). When I became involved in the Walk to Emmaus program (introduced in Chapter 1), I came to appreciate the medium of storytelling even more. Hearing other people's stories told in a Christian context helped me to be more aware of my experiences. It also made me become even more reflective in how I viewed virtually every input I received.

Teaching is a very powerful way of communicating, but the intended receiver needs to be in the mode of processing what is being presented. Jesus was, to my way of thinking, the best teacher that ever lived. He was called "Rabbi" (which means teacher), but there were several occasions where it was noted that He "spoke with authority" (Matthew 7:29). After all, who wants to spend their valuable time listening so someone blather on? He did have an advantage we don't have: He could read people's hearts. I don't know of anyone else that I can truthfully say that they can do that. Maybe some can read people's minds, and that is a good thing. We can acquire some skills that will help in that regard as I noted earlier in this chapter when we looked at *Emotional Intelligence.*

It seems that most of what Jesus was here for was to model behavior we should use when we are discipling others. He certainly pointed out the importance of His audience learning from him (Matthew 26:11 and Luke 10:38-42). Since the *Great Commission* commands us to make disciples, what Jesus left us with should be a great start. Certainly, Jesus used many methods to model. He used preaching for sure, and His disciples learned and did that well. In doing so, He also used stories and parables to illustrate important messages. He healed the maladies of many, and some of those gifts were passed on to His disciples. He also acted in ways intended to fulfill the Scriptures; but they were, in many cases, intended to model behavior as well. It seems to me communication was a bit of a challenge for some, and many left the crowd following Him because their hearts were not ready for His messages.

We are not told why these people left Jesus, but many of His rather cryptic stories and messages were even tough for His disciples. It was faith that kept them following Him, but we remember Peter denied Jesus three times and Thomas needed special evidence to be convinced. My point is we need to use all the forms of communication at our disposal to reach people for Christ. However, we must remember, in the end, it is the work of the Holy Spirit in willing hearts that will cause communication to occur.

We all know closeness is not necessarily a condition that comes automatically or by inheritance. Many of us have siblings we are not close to or even parents for that matter. It is always sad when that happens because the same blood runs through us. Today, marriage doesn't seem to have the bond it once had. Most of all, relationships require effort from the partners, but it would be better if we went into them with the right attitude. As was mentioned at the beginning of this chapter, determining what is important to the other party can go a long way toward making a relationship happen. We are not in this by ourselves, and relationships can make situations work.

What I am suggesting is that we humble ourselves, and it is not easy for most of us. We can never have a meaningful relationship if it is all about us. \

Appendix questions:

1. How can we develop better means of *filtering* that enable us to discern what is being conveyed in the communications we receive?

2. What impact do you think the era of mass communication has had on understanding?

3. What are the ways we can use communication to build relationships?

Appendix I

INTENTIONALITY

Unfortunately for me, my most vivid understanding of "intent" comes from the language in an IRS audit. When explaining the basis for disclaiming a deduction, the statement to explain it begins "It was not the *intent* of Congress" and then goes on to state what Congress' *intent* was not. I've been audited several times. From what I came to understand, the reason that folks like me have been "targeted" by IRS computers is I have a double whammy going for me: 1) I own a small business and 2) I have extensive travel involved as part of my work. That makes sense to me because I had only been audited once before owning my own business, and that was because the IRS found a savings account my wife had when we got married. I wasn't even aware of it – she had forgotten about it herself.

So, it seems to me while the *intent* of Congress was one thing, the *intent* of the IRS was to single out certain taxpayers and to go for what they generally find to be fertile ground for auditors. After being audited three times in a 6-year period, I began to ascertain the real intention for going after certain targets. Unfortunately, the IRS can lift things on an audit with their accusations, and the taxpayer has to prove their innocence. I don't wish that on anyone. My point is *intent* is a crucial factor in determining whether a person or persons has acted in accordance with the law. The importance of this is: how do we influence the intention of those we are trying to lead in the right direction?

Different people do things for a variety of different reasons. That's pretty obvious, but it does matter why you do something. We sometimes don't really know why we do them; we just keep on doing them the same way. Isn't that the definition of insanity that I shared in Appendix D – doing the same thing over and over again and expecting different results? Well, not exactly. Sometimes we do them the same way because we do want the same results. I love the story about the woman who was helping her mother prepare Easter dinner and asked her mother why she always cut the end of the ham off before she put it in the pan. She replied that her mother always did it that way. The daughter wanted to know the reason Grandma did that. Her mother said she didn't know but they could ask Grandma who was sitting in the other room. Grandma's reason was the hams she bought were always too big for the pans she used to cook them in.

While heredity does make a difference in determining the inclination of an individual, environment also has an important part to play. Parents, friends, teachers, leaders of organizations you are involved in, all of these have an influence on how you fashion your thinking about things. You may be viewing this with a little bit of skepticism considering the "rebellious" nature of younger generations. Consider that there is such a thing as negative influence. If you are one of the non-rebellious types, you may find this a bit obtuse. However, you probably know someone that did just the opposite of what they had been told that they should do with their lives. Rather than falling in with what the family had been doing (like being a doctor or whatever), they were repulsed by the notion of dealing with the lifestyle of that occupation (like blood or vomit). Nonetheless, cognitive dissonance drives people to what they really want to do. So, what I'm getting at is: we are wired for something. We have talents – things like singing or acting – and we have gifts. You may argue that singing and acting are gifts for some people. Sure, but many, many more people can sing or act than are talented enough to be called "gifted." A good example of how talent and giftedness can interact with each other is provided in *In His Steps* by Charles Sheldon (Sheldon 2010, 188). It is a novel, but the stories are very realistic. The one that illustrates my point is about a woman who had a great career opportunity as a singer and gave it up to stay in the neighborhood and help needy people. She used her gift/talent as a singer, but she mainly helped the residents with their needs. It happens more than you might think.

For some people, it takes a lifetime to learn your calling. It certainly did for me. My parents wanted me to be a preacher as my grandfather was, but I didn't know it until later in life. I'm pretty sure they didn't think I wanted to do that. Due to my "giftedness" in math and an affinity for construction, I planned to be a civil engineer and enrolled in classes that would prepare me for that career path. However, the first course I took in that field convinced me I needed a different path. I decided on law school, but I went through several majors in my undergraduate studies. When I changed my mind about law school, my major was Marketing. I went into the U.S. Air Force directly after graduation still not knowing exactly what I wanted to do with my life. When that was over, I started a career in business and I never left the field.

The reason I share this is people used to stay in a career for most of their lives. I actually thought about staying in the Air Force and changed due to the uncertainties of being in the military during a time of war. I met a man at a seminar who said he couldn't imagine being in one job for five years. I thought he must be a malcontent, but the only time I stayed in one that long was when I worked for myself. So, where's the *intent* in a career like mine? It has been said we have to live life forward, but we can only understand it by looking backward. I can now see, whatever job I had, my *intent* has always been to be of service in some way. Interest and aptitude tests have borne that out for me, but specific jobs weren't so clearly identified.

Much of what I have done has involved people. It's hard to teach effective people skills from what I have come to understand. For instance, I spent most of my career in sales of some sort. If you spend your efforts trying to make people like you or your company, you are not seeking the correct outcome. Certainly, there are aspects of the sales process that require you to develop a relationship with your potential customer. This has been a recurring theme, and I especially address it in Appendix C. I've had salespeople who called on me as well as prospects I had a friendship with. We never developed a relationship because what I was selling or buying didn't fit what they had or needed. We developed a friendship because I was sensitive to their needs and didn't keep trying to sell them anything. As a result, there were occasions when I was able to sell them something later because I kept calling on them.

It is my belief my working life has been a learning experience with regard to how to live up to my calling to serve people. Dr. Charles Stanley once said that there are two kinds of people (of course there are): those who live to be served and those who live to serve. With the experiences I had, it seems to me my time in business endeavors, including consulting with business owners and owning my own businesses, prepared me to be a mentor to small business owners. In addition, my penchant for justice (wanting to be a lawyer) is now being served by seeking to help those who are being overlooked by the "system." This has been my *intent* all along.

So, here's the point: it is best to determine what your intent is before you engage in an activity. Christian Schwarz, in his section on *Sustainability* (Schwarz 2012, 76-77) says there are two different focal points for projects: 1) he calls "Box A" which describes the resources required to reach an objective and 2) "Box B" which describes the results that you want to achieve. He accurately points out most leaders that are successful (by the culture's standards) focus mostly on "Box A." In other words, they make it their intention to garner as many resources as they can. Many times, they lose sight of what the real goal should be: results. If their intention were to get results, they would only look at Box A as a means to the end.

Intentionality will determine the outcome if you are true to it. Without it, you may find yourself just going through the motions and probably not accomplish much. Jim Collins' great, best-selling book, *Good to Great*, is a wonderful portrayal of the difference between companies that succeed at Box A and become good, and the ones that focus on Box B and become great. Most of the time, the *great* companies are not recognized as being so. You see, what I alluded to earlier about the culture is quite true. Leaders, no matter what the organizational setting might be, get recognized more for things that really don't have much to do with real success. This is more the case with nonprofits or other volunteer organizations. Raising money, building edifices, recruiting lots of volunteers; these are all good for organizations by culture's standards. They may generally be beneficial, but in themselves they don't do anything to achieve the purpose of the organization.

Here's where we see the reason for determining the benefit (one of the meanings of profit) of those things you take on. Clarity of goals is of extreme importance because, if we can "see" what it is that we are aiming for, we have a better chance of hitting it.

This might be a good point to take another look at *calling* regarding being intentional. I've spent a good deal of the past twenty years working to ascertain God's call on my life. I mentioned earlier in Chapter 1 about the change that reading *Found: God's Will* made in my life. The reality is that it means many things depending on the person's own situation. It took a second reading for me to get the full meaning it conveyed.

So, here's where my search led me: God's will comes to different people in different ways. We must learn to discern His message from all the "noise" that we are bombarded with. One of the ways we do that is to "look and listen" to what is coming at you. It is my experience that God is sending messages to us all the time. There are some ways you can discern the message from them; you just need to pray and study. There are some excellent materials available that can help you. As you do these things, you will be led by the Holy Spirit.

One thing you can do that will be very helpful is to take a Spiritual Gifts Assessment. (Where have you heard that before?) They measure things a little differently depending on which one you choose. If the one you use is part of a "system," you will be guided in ways to live out the calling you are gifted for. Christian Schwarz's Natural Church Development program is very broad-reaching and can be helpful as a church-wide solution as well.

One of my favorite Christian writers, Carlo Carretto, in *Letters from the Desert* (Carretto 1972, 73), provided this:

Whether you are on the sand worshipping, or at the teacher's desk in a classroom, what does it matter as long as you are doing the will of God?

And if the will of God urges you to seek out the poor, to give up all you possess, or leave for distant lands, what does the rest matter? Or if it calls you to found a family or take a job in a city, why should you have any doubts?

"His will is our peace," says Dante. And perhaps that is the expression which best brings into focus our deep dependence on God.

Max Lucado wrote a small but powerful book entitled *Live to Make a Difference* (Lucado 2010, ix-xii). His *intent*, as I see it, is to make it "An inspiring call to action" as the subtitle states. He introduces us to 120 or so people who appear in Acts 1:15 as the Jerusalem church. Amazing results were accomplished through these people who represented many different walks of life. Lucado questions whether God would do with us as He did with Jesus' first followers.

In considering an answer to this question he cites some startling statistics. This was written in 2010, but my sense is that it hasn't gotten any better: one billion people are hungry, millions are trafficked in slavery, pandemic diseases are gouging entire nations, and nearly two million children exploited in the global commercial sex trade every year. He doesn't stop there, but the point is that there are certainly a lot of problems in our world today. The sad reality is many that die every year could have been saved by one shot! Additionally, he says 2% of the world's grain harvest (if shared) would be enough to erase the problems of hunger and malnutrition around the world.

Lucado writes this:

No one can do everything, but everyone can do something. Some people can fast and pray about social sin. Others can study and speak out. What about you? Why not teach an inner-city Bible study? Use your vacation to build homes in hurricane-ravaged towns? Run for public office? Help a farmer get an ox?

What impresses me about Lucado's suggestions is none of these are focused on activities for their own sake: they are focused on results that make a difference (as his book title states). There are also two of these suggestions that fit the pattern of how I am led to contribute to the change that is necessary to help alleviate poverty and despair. The first is the suggestion to study and speak out. This is something I have been engaged in for several years. It was at once an exhilarating and a frustrating journey. This book is the culmination of my attempt to speak out in a dramatic way.

The other suggestion is to "Help a farmer get an ox." Lucado shares a story about doing just that, but it is not the specific endeavor that is important. This is the business of micro-financing that has become so meaningful in the developing world. Encouraged in no small part by Ben Newell with the Cooperative Baptist Fellowship, I have sought to shape a ministry that will encourage entrepreneurs to start businesses in declining rural areas and urban neighborhoods. A key to this happening in a meaningful way is to have realistic financing as a component. Unless something changes in the coming years to improve the current situation, micro-financing will become more important to small businesses. However, it must be coupled with incentives that will help keep the debt as low as possible. I dealt with this more in Appendix E.

Going back to the point I made earlier regarding goal setting; I want to re-emphasize the importance of being able to have a vision about what you intend to achieve. The word *vision* implies that you can "see" the intended outcome as if it were a reality. When we "see" it, we can become intentional about doing what it takes to accomplish the desired ends.

Appendix questions:

- Have you ever done something that didn't turn out the way you intended?

- What should we do if we *intend* to do God's will and we fail trying?

- How important is it to be intentional about things you are involved in?

- Is creating a plan the same as intending to do something?

APPENDIX J

ENTREPRENEURSHIP IN AMERICA

Entrepreneurship was not invented in America, but it quickly became the greatest creator of entrepreneurial activity in the world. The extreme irony in this incredible growth came out of the "invasion" of people, primarily from Europe, into the "New World." This might be a good point at which to define entrepreneurship in its most used description. The term is used to cover a "multitude of sins" and is often thought of in a negative connotation.

Author, speaker, and radio and TV personality, Dave Ramsey, wrote a book called *Entreleadership* (Ramsey 2011, 9). Ramsey is best known for his personal financial advice, but he is certainly an entrepreneur as well. The best advice is given by one who has lived the life of whatever it is that he/she is commenting on. His definition is: Someone who organizes, operates, and assumes risk for a venture. This comes from the word *Entreprendre* – one who takes risk. Here are some words Ramsey uses to expand on his definition:

Risk taker	Out of the box	Driven	Motivated
Visionary	Determined	Work ethic	Learner
Passionate	Courageous	Creative	Maverick

Notice that most of these don't necessarily describe people who invent things. To be fair, some entrepreneurs are quite innovative, but most innovators are more focused on developing products or services that are different from those already available. Entrepreneurs are more like enterprisers in that they are the folks who can get to market with innovations and take the risk for being successful or not. I won't go into examples of situations, but I have observed and worked with those who have created something that needs to be taken to market. They really do need an entrepreneur to get them into the stream of commerce.

Don't think that I am splitting hairs with this; it seems that too many people think the world is waiting for their innovation. They feel like all they must do is to come up with a "great idea" and do a little advertising. Even with the ability to patent or copyright something, there are those who are just waiting to pounce on other's ideas and make a successful run with it. That makes innovators very vulnerable. Mark Zuckerberg's experience in getting Facebook going is an example of how crazy situations can go. Obviously, it came out OK for him, but a lot of people were hurt in the process. He is considered an entrepreneur because he ultimately made it a success.

Franchises are a way that entrepreneurs can *make it*. Many people would argue that this isn't entrepreneurship, and perhaps it is not a fair characterization. Those folks don't know what it is like getting into a *packaged plan*. If you have significant experience in the business field you are getting involved in, you are possibly taking less of a risk. Also, if you are purchasing an existing business, you may be able to minimize your risk. However, I was a partner in a business that ended up closing that was an existing business. None of us knew the business and were relying on the manager and employees that stayed after the purchase.

The great business guru, Tom Peters (Peters 1989), wrote in *A Passion for Excellence*, that CEO's and the like must reinvent themselves and/or their business after about six years. This is because stagnation sets in just about that time. A business must be a fit for the owner, so it makes perfect sense to shape it to fit your passions and vision. In such cases, some innovation and creativity are needed. If entrepreneurs are good at sensing an opportunity, they can get a leg up on people who are *one-trick ponies*. It is the real value they bring to the table unless they are backing someone who is doing the work.

Innovation is the key to our economic future. It is the only source of sustainable growth. Spin-offs that come from innovative business ventures account for many start-up businesses. In much of history, large gaps in wealth have been followed by massive surges in innovation. This may be due to a sense of being left behind. The U.S. has a very good system that supports innovation, and it needs to be revived. Young minds need to think more about entrepreneurship than working in corporate America. I recently heard on the business news that only 24% of the new entrepreneurs are in the age range of 20 to 34. Ten years ago, the percentage was 34%.

The real missing component to economic success that will come from innovation is successful business models. This is where entrepreneurs come in. They are the ones that take ideas to market using these business models. The road to success is sometimes littered with poor business models that have been applied to winning ideas. It is not widely known that IBM was not an innovative company. They were just masters at finding where the ideas could flourish and creating a plan to get products/ideas into the hands of those that needed them.

The important point to take away from the above is the need for both innovators and entrepreneurs. Together they take new and approved ideas and turn them into successful ventures.

Some Background on Entrepreneurship in America

George Santayana (Santayana) said, "Those who cannot learn from history are doomed to repeat it." Early America was primarily an agricultural economy, and the exports reflected it. Entrepreneurship consisted of artisans and those who supported agriculture since England was the recipient of most of the exports. This moved into iron ore and later into cotton. England kept a tight rein on what was produced – only raw materials initially. Mercantilism, the practice countries used to accumulate gold by running trade surpluses, made economics become more of a political activity. While England kept a hold on every business activity of the colonies, there was a lot of freedom for the colonies due to the hold being a lax one. England's reaction to this was taxation, and we know where that led.

Gradually manufacturing began to be shifted to the colonies, due mainly to some surreptitious activities. The Industrial Revolution and the Louisiana Purchase worked together to create a population explosion of sorts. Since cotton and other agricultural products came from the South and the manufacturing was mainly done in the North, transportation became very important. Ocean and inland shipping and railroads were mainly owned by Northerners and the South's economy was tied to land and slave labor costs, the balance of capital was clearly vested in the North. Through many years of strife, the Civil War (War Between the States, as the South called it) settled the matter of whether the capital remaining in the South would allow the area to rebound. Eventually, through banking crises and other travails, the tables began to balance somewhat. American ingenuity and determination helped to carry the country through two World Wars and two Asian conflicts. The freedom to innovate (and to fail at it) is the main reason that America has made it through many ups and downs.

Impact on American Entrepreneurship Going Forward

A lot of this Appendix is dealing with how the history of the U.S. has impacted the lot of entrepreneurs in specific and business in general. The reason I mention both is people can be entrepreneurs and not be a businessperson, *per se*. Tom Peters (Peters 1989) described people within an organization who act like entrepreneurs. He called them *intrapreneurs*, and one of the examples he used was a group in a large corporation that were referred to as *Skunkworks*. Under the definition that I used at the beginning of this chapter, they would more likely be innovators. Peters wasn't trying to argue the point, as I recall. He was trying to show how people who are innovative can be put to good use in a bureaucracy and not be looking to take an idea out into the cold, cruel world of entrepreneurs. There have been some situations I am aware of where employees of a bureaucracy act like entrepreneurs. This is not generally permitted, though, because security is the only thing keeping them from going out on their own.

The concept of *social entrepreneurship* was introduced earlier in this book. It has some different connotations, but it is generally thought of as entrepreneurship in a non-profit setting. These entrepreneurs are basically like the ones we have come to know. That is, hopefully, the ones that I have described in this book. These are the ones that are involved in *social enterprises* – businesses that seek to make a difference – and they have a different drive to succeed. They are passionate, innovative, risk-tolerant, resourceful, and outcome-focused. They draw on knowledge bases that include both business and non-profit experiences.

Laurie Beth Jones, who wrote *Jesus, CEO*, also wrote, *Jesus, Entrepreneur* (Jones 2001, xiii-xxiv). While the former described the actions of Jesus as he modeled behavior important to His followers, the later dealt with people who work as entrepreneurs, but not in business. She called these folks *spiritreneurs*. She made an excellent case of how many people "color outside of the lines" in jobs not involved with operations considered to be businesses. There are lots of people who fit the spiritreneur description. They are commonly known as *social entrepreneurs*. They are probably not private business owners and may not even have business experience. While many of them are very donation-dependent, more and more are becoming self-sustaining. Far be it from me to disparage the largess of well-meaning folks who donate to charitable organizations. These donations may involve time as well as money or other tangibles such as food. However, I am of the school that believes people should do for themselves if at all possible. I spent a lot of time on that in various places in the book, and I don't intend to here. I do, however, want to show the similarities between the two types of entrepreneurs as they relate to government activities.

A primary reason for writing this book is to do what I can to help bring some sanity to how efforts to revitalize failing communities are done. Lupton (Lupton 2010, 31-49) believes in a theological balance to our understanding of wealth. It was this concept that helped spark my interest in what this book covers, especially Chapter 2. As a businessperson, I have struggled with the way that clergy and non-business Christians "do" charity. I've been over this in great detail already, so I just want to point out here that we need to be on the same page to really see significant change. Lupton is hoping that churches will have resourced members step up, and that they will see themselves as more than just saving souls. He believes – as do I – that churches can also be a catalyst for just and fruitful economies. Businesspeople need to see themselves as important players, using their skills as gifts from God to enable them to do well and to do good at the same time.

A couple of differences need to be a part of this process to help these *spiritreneurs* stand out as a major part of the solution. First is the notion of help vs. investment. In Chapter 8 I wrote about the difference in how their source of funding is constructed: donor model vs. cyclical model. Second, it creates a new type of corporate structure that encourages ethical behavior. This means the focus is on more than profit-making. These are the key elements that will enable the funding of social ventures to create jobs and wealth.

Here's where I start to plow a bit "closer to the corn". One of the notions that has been behind a lot of what I am trying to do in building community, is that Christian denominations, for the most part, are just not that interested in tackling the role that money/wealth must play in this matter. In Chapter 2, I addressed the situation insofar as folks understanding what *profit* actually is. Dr. Phil McGraw, in his book, *Life Strategies: Doing What Works, Doing What Matters*, provides Ten Laws of Life. One of them is "People Do What Works." My understanding of this is that people find a way to do what makes a difference in being successful. With all due deference to Dr. Phil, that is exactly what I believe is behind the separation between entrepreneurs – businesspeople and others – and the church when the subject comes up. We aren't all driven by the same motivations, and entrepreneurs are a determined breed. *Greed*, one of the Seven Deadly Sins, is generally applied to money/wealth in general and to businesspeople in particular. It is hard to make any progress when no one wants to give any ground or maybe even dialog about it.

So then, here we are. There's no real interest in forming a community. People are so out for themselves that they can't see that we are all in this together. Rural towns and declining city neighborhoods are struggling because their economic base is fading away if not already gone. Citizens are fearful, but they are just trying to survive. The sad reality is that the world is not waiting for their wishes to come true. Something must be done.

Appendix questions:

- Do you think that there is (or should be) a strong relationship between innovators and entrepreneurs?
- How do you feel about the importance of entrepreneurs in making our economy strong?
- Is there the same responsibility for social entrepreneurs as there is for for-profit entrepreneurs?
- How can entrepreneurs be the catalyst to revitalize a community?

REFERENCE LIST

Angelou, Maya. https://www.goodreads.com/quotes/663523-at-the-end-of-the-day-people-won-t-remember-what

Augustine of Hippo, 398. Confessions, quote provided by Good Reads, https://www.goodreads.com/quotes/42572-thou-hast-made-us-for-thyself-o-lord-and-our.

Bailey, Kenneth, 2008. Jesus Through Middle Eastern Eyes, (Downers Grove, IL, InterVarsity Press)

Berra, Yogi. https://www.brainyquote.com/authors/yogi_berra

Bonhoeffer, Dietrich, The Cost of Discipleship, (New York, Macmillan, 1966) excerpt by Shane Vander Hart, Caffeinated Thoughts, June 3, 2010, https://caffeinatedthoughts.com/2010/06/dietrich-bonhoeffer-cheap-grace-vs-costly-grace/

Cain, Herman, 2016. interview on Fox and Friends, Fox News Channel, https://www.foxnews.com/on-air/fox-and-friends

Camus, Albert https://www.goodreads.com/quotes/search?utf8=%E2%9C%93&q=camus+evil&commit=Search

Carretto, Carlo, 1975. Letters from the Desert, (Longman and Todd Ltd.), as quoted in Rueben P. Job and Norman Shawchuck, A Guide to Prayer for All God's People. Nashville, TN, Upper Room, 1990.

Chesterton, G.K., 1905, Heretics, (independently published, April 25, 2017), as quoted by Good Reads, https://www.goodreads.com/quotes/166354-truth-of-course-must-of-necessity-be-stranger-than-fiction.

Churchill, Winston https://www.goalcast.com/2017/06/20/top-24-winston-churchill-quotes-to- inspire-you-to-never-surrender/. https://quoteinvestigator.com/2014/02/24/heart-head/

Clifton, Jim, 2011. The Coming Jobs War: What Every Leader Must Know About the Future of Job Creation. New York: Gallup Press.

Collins, Jim, 2001. Good to Great: Why Some Companies Make the Leap... and Others Don't, Harper Collins. https://en.wikipedia.org/

wiki/Good_to_Great.

Colson, Charles. https://www.christianquotes.info/quotes-by-author/chuck-colson-quotes/?listpage=2&instance=2#participants-list-2

Crosby, Phillip, 1980. Quality Is Free, (New York, Penguin)

D'sousa, Dinesh 2008. "What's So Great about Christianity", Tyndale House Pub. http://www.azquotes.com/quotes/topics/servant-leadership.html?p=2

Drucker, Peter, 1995, Managing in Times of Great Change, (New York: Truman Talley Books/Dutton). https://en.wikipedia.org/wiki/Peter_Drucker.

Eberstadt, Nicholas, 2016. Men Without Work: America's Invisible Crisis. W. Conshohocken PA: Temple Press.

Farber, Steve, 2009, Greater Than Yourself: The Ultimate Lesson in True Leadership, (Doubleday)

Friedman, Milton, 1993, Why Government Is the Problem, (Stanford University, Hoover Institution Press)

Gladwell, Malcolm, 2000, The Tipping Point: How Little Things Can Make a Difference, (Little Brown).

Giuliani, Rudolph, 2008 Don Imus radio program.

Hill, Napoleon, 2004. Think and Grow Rich. New York: Jeremy P. Tarcher/Penguin.

Hendrickson, William. Essentials for Growth in Godliness, Part 1 https://www.gty.org/library/sermons-library/50-5, March 15, 1988

Huckabee, Mike, 2016, interview on Fox and Friends, Fox News Channel, https://www.foxnews.com/on-air/fox-and-friends

Hybels, Bill, 2007, Holy Discontent: Fueling the Fire that Ignites Personal Vision, (Zondervan)

Jones, Laurie Beth, 2001, Jesus, Entrepreneur: Using Ancient Wisdom to Launch and Live Your Dreams. New York: Three Rivers Press.

Kaufman Foundation, 2015. https://www.kauffman.org/what-we-do/resources/entrepreneurship-policy-digest/the-importance-of-young-firms-for-economic-growth

Keynes, John Maynard https://en.wikipedia.org/wiki/John_Maynard_Keynes

Krauthammer, Dr. Charles, 2009, interview on Special Report, Fox News Channel, https://www.foxnews.com/on-air/special-report

Liar, Liar Universal Pictures 1997.

Lemonis, Marcus, 2016, The Profit, CNBC Network.

Logan, Robert and Tara Miller, 2007. From Followers to Leaders, St. Charles, IL: ChurchSmart.

Lucado, Max, 2010. Live to Make a Difference: An Inspiring Call to Action, Nashville: Thomas Nelson.

Lupton, Robert, 2011, Toxic Charity: How Churches and Charities Hurt Those They Help (and How to Reverse It) New York, Harper One; 2015. Charity Detox: What Would Charity Look Like if We Cared About Results. New York, Harper One.

MacArthur, Dr. John, 1972, Found God's Will, (David C. Cook)

Mayer, Paul, 2002, Unlocking Your Legacy: 25 Keys for Success. Chicago, Moody Press.

Maxwell, John, 2000. Failing Forward: Turning Mistakes into Stepping Stone for Success.Nashville:Thomas Nelson.

McCullough, Donald, 1995. The Trivialization of God: The Dangerous Illusion of a Manageable Deity. Colorado Springs, CO, Nav Press.

McGraw, Phil, 1999. Life Strategies: Doing What Works, Doing What Matters. New York Hyperion Books.

McLennan, Scotty and Laura Nash, 2001. Church on Sunday, Work on Monday: The Challenge of Fusing Christian Values with Business Life. San Francisco, Jossey-Bass.

Millan, Cesar 2017. https://en.wikipedia.org/wiki/Cesar_Millan

Mises, Ludwig Von, 1956. The Anti-capitalistic Mind.

Morley, Patrick, 1999. Second Half for the Man in the Mirror. (Grand Rapids: Zondervan)

New York Times. https://www.nytimes.com/2017/07/20/opinion/finland-universal-basic-income.html

Paige, Satchel. https://www.brainyquote.com/authors/satchel_paige

Palotta, Dan. http://www.ted.com/talks/dan_pallotta_the_way_we_think_about_charity_is_dead_wrong

Pascal, Blaise, 1669. https://en.wikipedia.org/wiki/Pascal%27s_Wager

Peter, Dr. Lawrence, 1969. The Peter Principle: Why Things Always Go Wrong. William Morrow and Company. https://www.brainyquote.com/authors/laurence_j_peter".

Peters, Tom, 1989. A Passion for Excellence: The Leadership Difference, Grand Central Publishing.

Psychology Today. https://www.psychologytoday.com/us/basics/emotional-intelligence March 22, 2017

Reagan, Ronald, 2004. https://www.brainyquote.com/authors/ronald_reagan

Rohn, Jim, 2018. https://www.jimrohn.com/change-can-change-life/

Roosevelt, Theodore. https://www.brainyquote.com/authors/theodore_roosevelt. http://www.azquotes.com/quotes/topics/servant-leadership.html 2015.

Santayana, George. https://en.wikiquote.org/wiki/George_Santayana

Schwarz, Christian, 2006. Natural Church Development: A Guide to Eight Essential Qualities of Healthy Churches. St. Charles, IL: ChurchSmart Resources.

Shaw, George Bernard. https://www.goodreads.com/quotes/8202-the-mass-of-men-lives-of-quiet-desperation-what

Sinek, Simon. http://www.ted.com/talks/simon_sinek_how_great_leaders_ inspire_action.September 2009.

Stanley, Dr. Charles, 2008. https://www.intouch.org/ - radio broadcast

Smick, David M., 2017. The Great Equalizer: How Main Street Capitalism Can Create an Economy for Everyone. Philadelphia: Perseus Books.

Walker, Jay, 2016. http://www.glennbeck.com/audio/?format=radio

Walk to Emmaus. http://emmaus.upperroom.org/about

Warren, Rick, 2002. The Purpose Driven Life: What on Earth Am I

Here For? Grand Rapids: Zondervan

Wiesel, Elie. https://www.goodreads.com/quotes/tag/philosophy

Williams, Rev. Michael E. 2017. Everyone Is a Storyteller, The Interpreter 61, no. 3 (May-June), 40-41.

Willimon, William. 1978. The Gospel for the Person Who Has Everything. (Judson Press)

Zacharias, Ravi, 2012. Why Jesus: Rediscovering His Truth in an Age of Mass Marketed Spirituality. New York: FaithWords

www.ingramcontent.com/pod-product-compliance
Lightning Source LLC
Chambersburg PA
CBHW040850210326
41597CB00029B/4796